America ★ the ★ Beautiful

How to Use This Book

Look for these special features in this book:

SIDEBARS, **CHARTS**, **GRAPHS**, and original **MAPS** expand your understanding of what's being discussed—and also make useful sources for classroom reports.

FAQs answer common **F**requently **A**sked **Q**uestions about people, places, and things.

WOW FACTORS offer "Who knew?" facts to keep you thinking.

TRAVEL GUIDE gives you tips on exploring the state—either in person or right from your chair!

PROJECT ROOM provides fun ideas for school assignments and incredible research projects. Plus, there's a guide to primary sources—what they are and how to cite them.

Please note: All statistics are as up-to-date as possible at the time of publication. Population data is taken from the 2010 census.

Consultant: William Loren Katz; Jon Emmett Purmont, Professor of History, Southern Connecticut State University; Robert Thorson, Center for Integrative Geosciences, University of Connecticut; Nancy Steenburg, Professor, University of Connecticut

Book production by The Design Lab

Library of Congress Cataloging-in-Publication Data
Kent, Zachary.
 Connecticut / by Zachary Kent. — Revised edition.
 pages cm. — (America the beautiful. Third series)
 Includes bibliographical references and index.
 ISBN 978-0-531-24879-9 (lib. bdg.)
 1. Connecticut—Juvenile literature. I. Title.
 F94.3.K47 2014
 974.6—dc23   2013031193

2 3 4 5 6 7 8 9 10 R 23 22 21 20 19 18 17 16 15 14

Connecticut

BY ZACHARY KENT

Third Series, Revised Edition

Children's Press®
An Imprint of Scholastic Inc.
New York ★ Toronto ★ London ★ Auckland ★ Sydney
Mexico City ★ New Delhi ★ Hong Kong
Danbury, Connecticut

CONTENTS

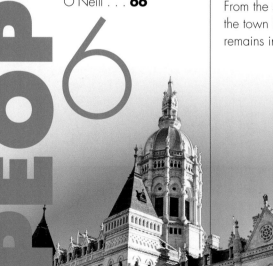

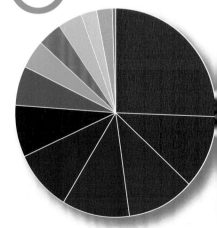

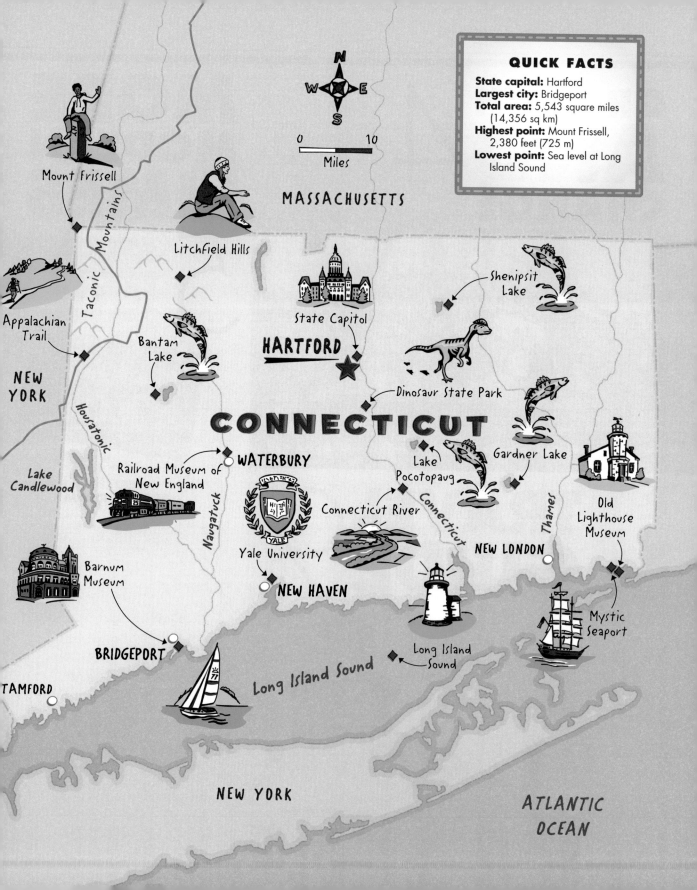

N W E S

0   10
Miles

MASSACHUSETTS

Mount Frissell

Litchfield Hills

Taconic Mountains

Appalachian Trail

NEW YORK

Bantam Lake

Housatonic

Lake Candlewood

State Capitol

HARTFORD

Shenipsit Lake

Dinosaur State Park

CONNECTICUT

Railroad Museum of New England

WATERBURY

Lake Pocotopaug

Gardner Lake

Naugatuck

YALE

Yale University

Connecticut River

Connecticut

Thames

Old Lighthouse Museum

NEW LONDON

Barnum Museum

NEW HAVEN

BRIDGEPORT

TAMFORD

Long Island Sound

Long Island Sound

Mystic Seaport

NEW YORK

ATLANTIC OCEAN

Welcome to Connecticut!

HOW DID CONNECTICUT GET ITS NAME?

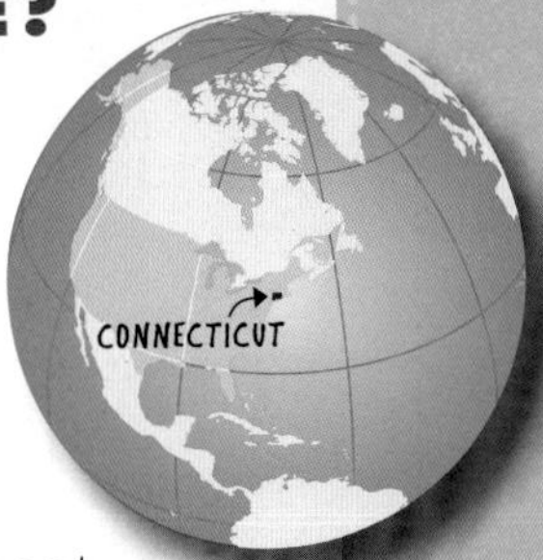

Through the center of Connecticut flows a wide and winding river. Its rolling waters have been giving life to the region since before recorded time. Native Americans of the Algonquian group hunted beside the river's shores and cast nets into the water to catch fish. They called the area *Quinnehtukqut*, meaning "beside the long tidal river." Later, English settlers cleared the river valley for farms. They relied on the river to provide power for mills and factories. The English kept the river's Native American name, but they spelled it Connecticut.

CONNECTICUT

ATLANTIC
OCEAN

8

READ ABOUT

A dense forest
surrounds Great
Pond in Simsbury.

LAND

★

CONNECTICUT MAY BE SMALL, BUT ITS LANDSCAPE IS FULL OF SURPRISES. WITHIN ITS BORDERS ARE COASTAL BEACHES, A FERTILE RIVER VALLEY, ROLLING HILLS, AND THICK WOODLANDS. Do not expect giant mountains, though. The highest point in the state is the southern slope of Mount Frissell at 2,380 feet (725 meters). The land drops to sea level on Long Island Sound at its lowest point. Its area of 5,543 square miles (14,356 square kilometers) is home to many different kinds of animals and plants.

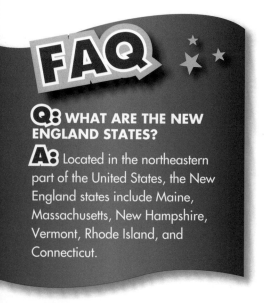

FAQ

Q: **WHAT ARE THE NEW ENGLAND STATES?**

A: Located in the northeastern part of the United States, the New England states include Maine, Massachusetts, New Hampshire, Vermont, Rhode Island, and Connecticut.

WORD TO KNOW

glacier *a large moving body of ice*

SCARS ON THE LAND

Imagine stepping into a time machine and traveling back 30,000 years. What would you find? In Connecticut, you would find yourself standing on top of a **glacier** almost 2 miles (3.2 km) thick! Centuries of cold weather caused a giant ice sheet to push south from the Arctic. Scientists call it the Wisconsin Glacier. It covered all of the New England states, including Connecticut, for at least 10,000 years. When it finally melted, the glacier left behind soil, gravel, boulders, and deep scars on the ground. The Wisconsin Glacier is responsible for the way Connecticut's surface looks today.

LAND REGIONS

Connecticut shares its northern border with Massachusetts. Cross the state line to the east and you will find yourself in Rhode Island. Cross the border to the west and you enter New York. Long Island Sound marks the state's entire southern border.

There aren't many states where you can swim in the ocean, canoe on a river, and climb a mountain—in the same day. But you can in Connecticut. There is plenty to see and do in each of Connecticut's four main land regions: the Taconic Mountains, the Central Valley, the Eastern and Western Uplands, and the Coastal Plain.

Connecticut Geo-Facts

Along with the state's geographic highlights, this chart ranks Connecticut's land, water, and total area compared to all other states.

Total area; rank	5,543 square miles (14,356 sq km); 48th
Land; rank	4,845 square miles (12,549 sq km); 48th
Water; rank	699 square miles (1,810 sq km); 37th
Inland water; rank	161 square miles (417 sq km); 47th
Coastal water; rank	538 square miles (1,393 sq km); 11th
Geographic center	Hartford, at East Berlin
Latitude	40° 58′ N to 42° 3′ N
Longitude	71° 47′ W to 73° 44′ W
Highest point	Mount Frissell, 2,380 feet (725 m)
Lowest point	Sea level at Long Island Sound
Largest city	Bridgeport
Number of counties	8
Longest river	Connecticut River

Source: U.S. Census Bureau, 2010 census

WOW Connecticut is small enough to fit inside Texas 48 times!

Connecticut Topography

Use the color-coded elevation chart to see on the map Connecticut's high points (dark red to orange) and low points (green to dark green). Elevation is measured as the distance above or below sea level.

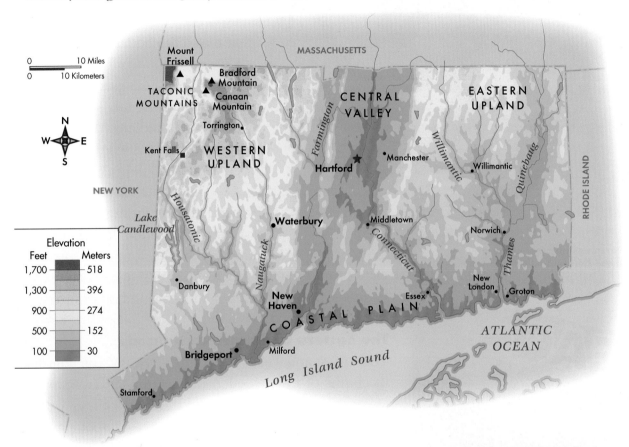

The Taconic Mountains

The Taconic Mountains fill the northwestern corner of Connecticut. Their peaks are part of the great Appalachian mountain range. Hikers travel along a section of the high Appalachian Trail, which passes through here. The southern slope of Mount Frissell, located in the towns of Mount Washington and Salisbury, marks the highest point in the state at 2,380 feet (725 m). On Mount Frissell lies a spot called Crying Child Rock. Legend has it that when the wind blows just right there, it sounds like a baby crying.

Potatoes and other crops grow in the Central Valley.

WORDS TO KNOW

depressed *sunken or in a lower position*

quarry *a place where stone is dug*

The Central Valley

"This River is a fine pleasant stream," wrote early Dutch visitor David de Vries in 1639, after gazing at the Connecticut River. The low Central Valley on both sides of the river extends north and south, nearly cutting the state in half. South of Middletown, where the river turns eastward, the valley continues following it southward.

The Connecticut River has been flowing for more than 10,000 years, ever since the great glacier melted. The soil is dark and fertile along the river. Each year, farmers collect rich Central Valley harvests of corn, potatoes, brussels sprouts, tobacco, and other crops.

The Eastern and Western Uplands

To the east and west of the Central Valley, the land rises in chains of low, wooded hills. Connecticut's uplands cover most of the state. From the river valley, the land slopes upward at the rate of about 12 feet per mile (2.3 m per km). Glacier water created more than 1,000 lakes where the land is **depressed**. Some of the largest natural lakes in Connecticut are Bantam, Pocotopaug, Gardner, Wangumbaug, and Shenipsit.

In western Connecticut, the uplands are commonly called the Litchfield Hills, named after Litchfield County. The soil of the uplands is thin and stony. Most farmers gave up trying to raise crops here long ago. In places, great hunks of solid bedrock push up from the ground. For years, **quarry** workers have cut upland stone for building blocks and have crushed it for road gravel.

The Coastal Plain

Where the land meets the sea: that is Connecticut's Coastal Plain. This strip of land ranges from 6 to 16 miles (10 to 26 km) wide and stretches some 253 miles (407 km) along the state's southern border. Of course, the shoreline is not straight. Add the wide bays and curving coves, river inlets and salty marshes, and you have a total coastline of about 583 miles (938 km). Sandy beaches make up nearly 79 miles (127 km) of this length. The beautiful views of Long Island Sound have attracted about 60 percent of Connecticut's residents to live along the coast of the region.

CLIMATE

"In the spring I have counted one hundred and thirty-six different kinds of weather inside of twenty-four hours," joked writer Mark Twain about Connecticut in 1876. Twain stretched the truth about the weather to get a laugh. Spend some time in the state, though, and you might agree with him. Connecticut may be small, but it has all kinds of weather.

What causes the weather patterns in Connecticut? Thanks to its **latitude** (40° 58' N to 42° 3' N), the state experiences all four seasons. Several different air-streams influence the state's weather, including cold, dry air from the north; warm air from the south; and cool, damp air from the northern Atlantic Ocean. Along the coast, summer temperatures are cooler and winter temperatures are warmer. Land elevation also affects the temperature. The greater the elevation, or height of the land, the cooler it gets. The coldest town in Connecticut is Norfolk in the northwestern uplands. There the average annual low temperature is 37 degrees Fahrenheit (2.8 degrees Celsius).

SEE IT HERE!

DRUMLINS

Do you want to see solid evidence that the great glacier passed through Connecticut? Put on your hiking shoes and climb a drumlin. Drumlins are low, oval hills made of sand, pebbles, and clay. They were left behind by the Wisconsin Glacier when it melted thousands of years ago. Connecticut has about 200 of these strange land features. They usually follow the same north to south direction that the ice sheet followed. In size, Connecticut's drumlins are never more than 1 mile (1.6 km) long and seldom more than 250 feet (76 m) high. Apple Hill in Glastonbury, Wickham Memorial Park and Veterans Memorial Park in East Hartford, Bailey Hill in Groton, and Jail Hill in Norwich are all fine examples of this unusual geography.

Weather Report

TEMPERATURE 106°F

TEMPERATURE -32°F

This chart shows record temperatures (high and low) for the state, as well as average temperatures (July and January) and average annual precipitation.

Record high temperature	106°F (41°C)
at Torrington on August 23, 1916, and at Danbury on July 15, 1995	
Record low temperature	–32°F (–36°C)
at Falls Village on February 16, 1943, and at Coventry on January 22, 1961	
Average July temperature	73°F (23°C)
Average January temperature	27°F (–3°C)
Average annual precipitation	.46 inches (117 cm)

Source: National Climatic Data Center, NESDIS, NOAA, U.S. Department of Commerce

Nor'easters

The wind is rattling the windows. A tall drift of snow is piling up against the house. You are in the middle of a nor'easter! Starting in the northern Atlantic Ocean, a strong current of cool, damp air moves in from the northeast. Sometimes the air current reaches hurricane force. New Englanders call these powerful storms nor'easters. A nor'easter that struck Connecticut in February 2013 dumped 22.8 inches (58 cm) of snow on Hartford, the second-highest total from a single storm in Hartford since records have been kept.

Tornadoes!

The clouds turn black. The wind starts howling. Lightning strikes and thunder booms. Connecticut gets

A man inspects his home after it was damaged during Hurricane Sandy in 2012.

between 18 and 35 thunderstorms each year. Some thunderstorms produce tornadoes. In 1878, 34 people died when a tornado suddenly struck the town of Wallingford. The area around Windsor suffered tornado damage of more than $215 million in 1979.

Hurricanes

If you live near the eastern or Gulf coasts of the United States, you have probably experienced a hurricane. Hurricanes originate over warm ocean waters and sometimes turn inland and create enormous damage on land. In October 2012, Hurricane Sandy slammed into the East Coast. In Connecticut, several people were killed and damages climbed above $360 million. More than half a million homes and businesses were without power for days. In August 2011, Hurricane Irene struck the region, causing immense damage and knocking out power in many areas.

PLANT LIFE

About 55 percent of Connecticut is covered with woods and forests. A study in Hartford County in 1885 counted 56 different kinds of trees, including elm, maple, oak, beech, and birch. Other common types found today are basswood, ash, hickory, hemlock, and

MINI-BIO

THOMAS COLE: LANDSCAPE PAINTER

Artist Thomas Cole (1801–1848), born in England, believed there was no place "more lovely or more peaceful than the valley of the Connecticut [River]." In his painting *The Oxbow* (1836), he captured a wonderful view of the river. You can see *The Oxbow* at the Metropolitan Museum of Art in New York City. Cole painted many other scenes of the Connecticut countryside, too.

? Want to know more? Visit www.factsfornow.scholastic.com and enter the keyword **Connecticut**.

Basswood tree in a field of dandelions

Connecticut has about 5,000 different kinds of wild plants. About 1,000—including ragweed and dandelions— were brought from Europe by the colonists.

GIFFORD PINCHOT: MANAGING THE FORESTS

Gifford Pinchot (1865–1946) was born in Simsbury. As a young man, he decided careful forest management should be a part of U.S. national policy. He was the first to use the word conservation to mean the protection of natural resources. In 1905, President Theodore Roosevelt named him the first chief of the U.S. Forest Service. In 1907, Pinchot urged Roosevelt to set aside an additional 16 million acres (6.4 million hectares) of public land as national forests.

? Want to know more? Visit www.factsfornow .scholastic.com and enter the keyword **Connecticut**.

Macedonia Brook State Park in northwestern Connecticut

Connecticut National Park Areas

This map shows some of Connecticut's national parks, monuments, preserves, and other areas protected by the National Park Service.

MASSACHUSETTS

Torrington

Appalachian NST

Gaylordsville

Housatonic

NEW YORK

Farmington

Hartford

Willimantic

Quinebaug

Waterbury

Naugatuck

Connecticut

Thames

RHODE ISLAND

0   10 Miles
0   10 Kilometers

Danbury

Weir Farm NHS

New Haven

ATLANTIC OCEAN

National Park area
NHS   National Historic Site
NST   National Scenic Trail

Bridgeport

Long Island Sound

Stamford

NEW YORK

N
W   E
S

fir. On land where farms have been abandoned, cedar and white pine often grow. Plenty of wild rice still grows in the state's coastal marshlands.

ANIMAL LIFE

The forests of Connecticut provide homes for many wild animals. Wildcats, also known as bobcats, are still sometimes reported in the rocky hills. The red fox can be spotted quietly moving through the woods. Other more common animals in Connecticut include the squirrel, chipmunk, weasel, wild turkey, mink, skunk, raccoon, and opossum.

More than 100,000 white-tailed deer live throughout Connecticut. You can often see them nibbling the grass beside the roads and wandering through backyards. Farmers and gardeners do not like them because they also eat bushes, flowers, and crops. Moose are native to the area, but they aren't found in large numbers. Rabbits, woodchucks, porcupines, muskrats, black bears, coyotes, and beavers can be found in the state, as can amphibians, such as salamanders and frogs, and reptiles, such as snakes.

Bass, trout, pickerel, and carp are freshwater fish found in the state. With so much coastline, saltwater fish such as flounder, shad, porgy, and mullet are also common.

ENDANGERED SPECIES

Connecticut's woods and marshes are slowly disappearing to make way for development. As these lands become populated by humans, the state's wildlife becomes increasingly threatened. The list of endangered species in Connecticut is long. According to the state's Department of Energy and Environmental Protection, there are 603 species that are either endangered, threatened, or of special concern. These are just some of the endangered birds:

American bittern	Peregrine falcon
Bald eagle	Pied-billed grebe
Barn owl	Red-headed woodpecker
Black rail	Roseate tern
Common moorhen	Sedge wren
Grasshopper sparrow	Sharp-shinned hawk
King rail	Upland sandpiper
Long-eared owl	Vesper sparrow

Barn owl

PROTECTING CONNECTICUT'S ENVIRONMENT

Keeping the water clean is a major concern of Connecticut citizens. Each year, factories in the state produce millions of gallons of hazardous waste. Chemicals including paint thinners, cleaning chemicals, pesticides (insect killers), and herbicides (plant killers) can end up in the state's water supply. It is important that the state's rivers, lakes, and wells remain clean.

Making sure the air is clean is also important. Factory chimneys belch smoke, which passes into the air. In 1981, for example, the state's air did not pass U.S. government standards on 111 days. Automobile exhaust added to the air pollution problem. Today, the U.S. Environmental

The people of Connecticut try to keep beaches clean so everyone can enjoy them.

Visitors read about an exhibit at Dinosaur State Park.

ROCKY HILL DINOSAUR TRACKS

You never know what you will find when you dig into the earth. In 1966, a new state building was under construction in Rocky Hill. Suddenly, bulldozer operator Ed McCarthy uncovered some strangely marked rocks. The marks turned out to be 185-million-year-old dinosaur tracks. They had been preserved in the mud beside a prehistoric lake. Archaeologists soon dug up 1,500 tracks, which were given to museums. Another 500 excavated sets of tracks were covered with a dome to create Dinosaur State Park.

Most of the Rocky Hill tracks were made by a birdlike dinosaur called the *Coelophysis*. About 4 feet (1.2 m) long, it stood on three-toed feet and ate small reptiles and insects. The largest footprints at Rocky Hill were left by a type of *Eubrontes* dinosaur, perhaps the *Dilophosaurus*.

Protection Agency (EPA) and the Connecticut Department of Motor Vehicles enforce laws that aim to improve the quality of the state's water and air.

Save the Sound is a program supported by the Long Island Sound Study and National Fish and Wildlife Foundation. Its mission is to help clean up Connecticut's beautiful 300-mile (480 km) waterfront. To date, more than 11,000 volunteers have come together to remove roughly 90,000 pounds (41 metric tons) of trash. The International Coastal Cleanup (ICC) group also works to beautify the state's coastline. In the past 25 years, almost 9 million people from all over the world have come to remove more than 144 million pounds (65,000 metric tons) of trash from the shoreline. Anyone care for a swim?

READ ABOUT

Native Americans in Connecticut all descended from Paleo-Indians who traveled to the region more than 12,000 years ago.

c. 9000 BCE

First people reach the region

c. 5000 BCE
Archaic way of life gradually develops

◄ **c. 2000 BCE**

Native Americans begin building villages

CHAPTER TWO

FIRST PEOPLE

★

FROM MESHOMASIC MOUNTAIN TO THE TOWN OF PAWCATUCK, THE STATE'S LOCALES HIGHLIGHT THE AREA'S NATIVE AMERICAN HISTORY. The first people arrived in the Connecticut region around 11,000 years ago. Called Paleo-Indians, they are ancestors of the Algonquian peoples.

1500s
Pequots live in what is now Connecticut

1524 CE
First recorded sighting of Native Americans by Europeans

◄ **c. 1600**
As many as 26 Algonquian groups live in the region

PALEO-INDIANS

When the Paleo-Indians arrived in the region, it looked much different than it does today. It had little plant life, and it was colder because the Wisconsin Glacier had only recently retreated. Traveling in small groups, Paleo-Indians primarily followed and hunted large herds of animals, using their meat for food, bones for tools, and hides for clothing and shelter. As the climate warmed, the variety of plant life increased. Gradually, over the next few thousand years, the people in the region began to hunt smaller animals, gather more wild plants, and fish, adapting to the changes in the environment. These people, with several different means of finding food, are called Native Americans of the Archaic period.

Native American Peoples
(Before European Contact)

This map shows the general area of Native American peoples before European settlers arrived.

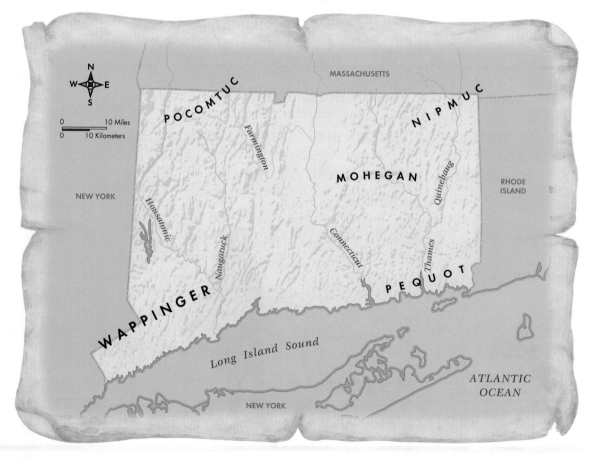

Villages and Shelters

Starting around 4,000 years ago, many of the people in the Connecticut region began living in larger groups and setting up seasonal villages. These groups had similar languages and cultures and are known as the Algonquian peoples. During the fall and winter, when it was cold, they lived in valleys and forests. There they were protected from icy winds, and firewood was plentiful. In the spring, when the days began to get warm, people packed their belongings and moved to camps along the rivers, lakes, and seacoast. In these open areas, there were cooling breezes, and food was plentiful.

Many Algonquian groups had a lot of things in common. The dwellings they built, the ways they hunted, and the clothes they wore were all similar. But as the area became more populated and settled, the different Algonquian groups fought one another for territory and over resources.

An Algonquian basket

FAQ

Q8 WHAT DOES ALGONQUIAN MEAN?

A8 People who study Native American cultures created the term *Algonquian* (sometimes spelled Algonkian). It describes a family of similar languages and the groups of Native peoples who speak them. The term is based on the word *Algonquin*, the name of one such group from what is now Canada.

THE PEQUOT

One of the many Algonquian-language speaking peoples of the region, the Pequot lived in eastern Connecticut, with main villages along the Connecticut and Thames rivers. Their villages were often located on hills and surrounded by palisades, fencelike protective structures made out of large posts. The Pequot battled for territory and goods, so it is no wonder they built defenses around their settlements.

The Algonquian peoples in the Connecticut region built dwellings called wigwams. Men cut young trees, or saplings, and trimmed them into long poles. They stuck the poles into the ground in a circle. When the opposite sapling tops were tied together, they created a domed frame. Women collected lengths of shredded tree bark or long reeds plucked from marshes. With these materials, they wove together mats. With bone needles and bark thread, they sewed the mats to the sapling frames. Spaces were left open for doorways, and a hole in the roof let smoke escape from the fire. Mat-covered wigwams kept people warm, dry, and comfortable. Native peoples sometimes built larger shelters, too, called longhouses, for more than one family. When people moved from one place to another, they took their wigwams apart and carried the rolled mats with them.

Algonquians construct wigwams.

GROWING CROPS

Corn was the most important crop for the region's Native peoples. But how did they grow it? First, the land had to be cleared. Men chopped down smaller trees with axes and hatchets. These tools had stone blades and wooden handles. They set fires at the bases of thick, large trees. Burned wood was easier to chop than live trees. Before long, only tree stumps could be seen on the cleared lands.

Now it was time to prepare the soil. To dig up the earth, they used shovels and hoes with stone or clam-shell blades and wooden handles. The dirt was piled in little mounds about 3 feet (90 centimeters) apart. To make the soil richer, they buried fish in the mounds as fertilizer. Then they planted four corn kernels in each mound. Often kidney beans were planted, too. Cornstalks rose beneath the summer sun. Bean vines attached themselves to the stalks and grew with them. Seeds of squash and pumpkins were also planted in the mounds. Their vines spread out between the mounds. Women tended these crops, while men looked after separate fields of planted tobacco. At harvesttime, the crops were collected in woven baskets.

SEE IT HERE!

THE MASHANTUCKET PEQUOT MUSEUM AND RESEARCH CENTER

Pequots have lived in Mashantucket in what is now eastern Connecticut for thousands of years. This museum contains a record of their history in the region. You'll find a replica of a 1500s Pequot village, as well as re-creations of a 1600s Pequot fort and a farm from the 1700s. They seem so real, you will think you have gone back in time. Climb 185 feet (56 m) to the top of the museum's observation tower and gaze out at the land Mashantucket Pequots still call home.

Squash

GOOD EATING!

Here are some familiar foods that were eaten by Algonquian peoples in Connecticut:

cornmeal	walnuts	bluefish
cornbread	blackberries	codfish
corn chowder	blueberries	halibut
hominy grits	cranberries	clams
popcorn	raspberries	crabs
baked beans	strawberries	lobsters
squash	watermelon	oysters
pumpkins	grapes	salmon
artichokes	plums	shad
chestnuts	roast turkey	shellfish

Bow and arrow

WORDS TO KNOW

sinew *the tough cord or tendon that connects muscles to bone*

breechcloth *a piece of cloth or leather worn at the lower body*

durable *long-lasting*

When Algonquian peoples in the Connecticut region got small cuts, they often would scoop up a spiderweb and press it against the wound. The web's stickiness could keep cuts closed!

HUNTING

After harvesttime, men spent the fall hunting. They tracked and killed wild game, as well as set traps to catch animals. Their arrows and spears had points of stone, shell, or sharpened bone. They carried their arrows in cone-shaped sacks, called quivers, mostly made of leather or woven bark. Wooden bows were between 5 and 6 feet (1.5 and 1.8 m) long. Animal **sinew** was stretched to make the bow strings.

After the hunt, nearly all parts of an animal were put to use. The meat was food—some to be eaten right away and some to be dried and stored for later use. Bones and antlers were rubbed against stones to sharpen them into knives and needles. Furs became blankets or hanging wigwam doors. Skins had many uses. Around campfires, women spent hours cutting skins and sewing them into clothes.

CLOTHES

The deerskin **breechcloth** was the most basic piece of men's clothing. About 48 inches (122 cm) long, it was secured with a belt around the hips. The ends hung down in front and back. Men wore deerskin leggings shaped like tubes that went from ankle to thigh. They

were held up with ties that fastened to their belt. Women wore shorter leggings that extended to their knees. On their upper bodies, men and women often wore capes, or mantles. These fastened over the left shoulder and hung under the right arm. Skins for cold-weather mantles had the fur attached. The fur side was worn against the body. On their feet, men and women wore moccasins made of moose skins, which are thick and **durable**.

A pair of moccasins

Connecticut Native Americans in the 1600s

This map shows the main Algonquian-speaking Native American groups remaining in Connecticut in the late 1600s and early 1700s

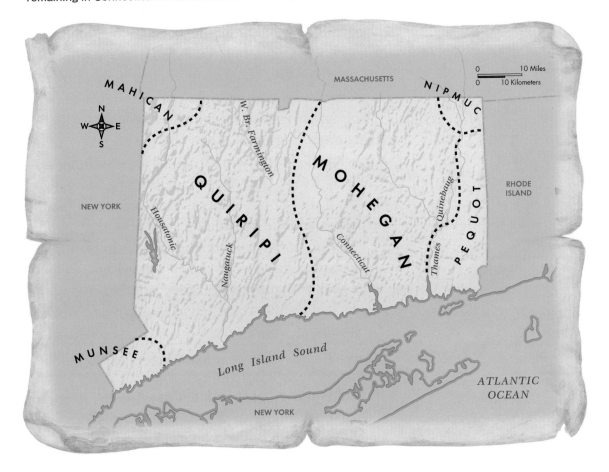

A painting from 1585 details a hairstyle commonly worn by Algonquian men along the Atlantic coast of North America.

APPEARANCE

Women wore their black hair in long braids. Men wore their hair in different ways. Some men wore braids. However, a single center strip of hair running from the front to the back of the head was the most popular style. Animal fat kept the short hair standing up stiffly. The sides of the head were shaved bare. Another style was to wear long hair on one side of the head and shave the other side clean. Some men completely shaved their heads except for one long braid of hair that hung down behind.

SPIRITUAL LIFE

The Algonquian peoples of the Connecticut region share similar spiritual beliefs. One story explains the creation of the earth and human beings this way: When the world was young, evil spirits sent a terrible flood to cover the earth. Some animals escaped to a high mountaintop in the southwest. The great god Cautantowit lived there. Some Algonquian groups called the great god by other names. The Quinnipiac called him Kiehtan, and others called him Woonand. Because they lived with Cautantowit, the escaped birds and beasts took on godlike qualities.

Cautantowit then remade the earth from mud. He tried to make a man and a woman out of stone. He was unhappy with these first people, so he smashed them to bits. He tried again and made a man and a woman from a living tree. This time, Cautantowit was pleased. He gave these people corn and beans to grow. He gave them rules to live by and other gifts such as wisdom, strength, and courage. After death, the souls of humans who lived good lives could journey to Cautantowit's southwest home. There they would live forever in peace and happiness.

On the earth, the spirits of the birds, beasts, and fish gave people hope and comfort each day. These spirits were called manitos. Each person chose a manito as a guide. People had a daily relationship with nature. This was because their manitos were always present in their dreams or in the sights and sounds of the forest. There was a sun spirit and a moon spirit. Another was the bird spirit who brought thunder, called the thunderbird. There was a house spirit and a fire spirit and spirits for the East, West, North, and South.

By the 1600s, there were at least 26 different Algonquian groups living in Connecticut. The way of life for each group was about to change dramatically and quickly.

SHAMANS

When you're sick, your doctor might prescribe medicine. The Algonquian peoples used natural cures, or remedies, made from bark, roots, and plants. They turned to shamans, also called spirit men or medicine men, for help when they were ill. The Algonquian peoples believed evil spirits caused diseases. A shaman was thought to have magical powers. For payment, he would try to get the evil spirit to leave. The sun spirit spoke when the shaman beat his drum. The moon spirit talked when the shaman shook his turtle shell rattle. The shaman danced and sang, shouted and howled. He blew into a wooden whistle and pulled stone charms from his medicine bag. The charms had pictures of animal spirits carved on them. These animal spirits served as helpers. At last, the shaman ended his dancing and shouting. It was hoped that the evil spirit had been persuaded to leave the patient's body.

Picture Yourself . . .

Playing Games with Mohegans

In winter, when snow covers the ground, you and your Mohegan friends play a game called snow snake. First, you clear a path, or trough, in the snow. Take your snow snake (a long stick with a bulge at one end that looks like a snake's head) and throw it down the trough. If you can make the stick slide farther than anyone else, you win!

30

READ ABOUT

Adriaen Block oversees the building of a ship in Narragansett Bay in the early 1600s.

1614
Adriaen Block sails up the Connecticut River

1636 ▲
Thomas Hooker arrives in the Connecticut Colony

1639
Fundamental Orders establish democratic colonial government

CHAPTER THREE

EXPLORATION AND SETTLEMENT

★

IN THE EARLY 1600S, THE LAND-SCAPE OF THE NATIVE PEOPLES IN CONNECTICUT BEGAN TO CHANGE AS EUROPEANS ARRIVED. In 1614, Dutch explorer Adriaen Block sailed up the Con-necticut River in his ship, the *Onrust*, which means "restless" in English. In 1633, Dutch trader Jacob Van Curler bought land from the Pequot and built a fort and trading post that stood where Hartford is now.

◄1662
Connecticut Colony is granted an official charter

1701
Yale College is founded

1775–1783
Connecticut citizens fight for American independence

European Exploration of Connecticut

The colored arrows on this map show the routes taken by explorers between 1632 and 1635.

THE FIRST EUROPEAN SETTLERS

It was the English, though, who came to Connecticut to stay. They were Puritans, a religious group of Protestant Christians. In search of freedom to practice their religion, many Puritans had left England in 1620. They established the Massachusetts Bay Colony on the Atlantic coast north of Connecticut in 1630. Soon after, English trading posts and farms took root at Windsor, Wethersfield, and

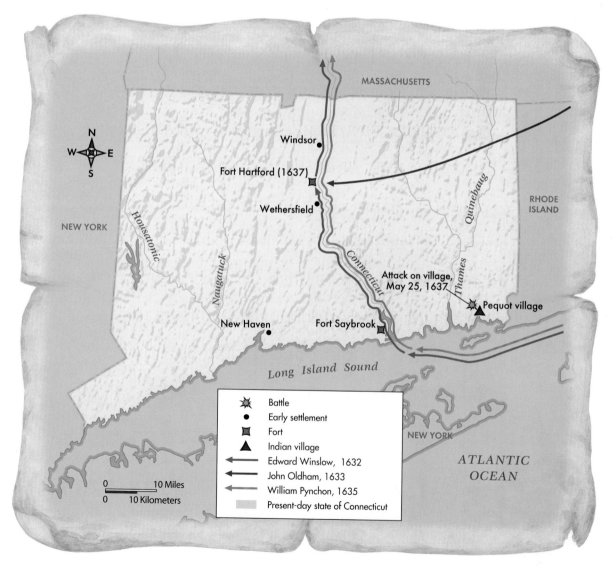

MASSACHUSETTS

Windsor

Fort Hartford (1637)

Wethersfield

NEW YORK

Housatonic

Naugatuck

Connecticut

Quinebaug

RHODE ISLAND

Thames

Attack on village, May 25, 1637

Pequot village

New Haven

Fort Saybrook

Long Island Sound

NEW YORK

ATLANTIC OCEAN

✺	Battle
●	Early settlement
⬟	Fort
▲	Indian village
←	Edward Winslow, 1632
←	John Oldham, 1633
←	William Pynchon, 1635
	Present-day state of Connecticut

0   10 Miles
0   10 Kilometers

Hartford. In 1636, these villages united to form the Connecticut Colony. Other settlements sprang up along the coast at places such as Quinnipiac (present-day New Haven and Hamden), Saybrook, Milford, and Stamford. They called themselves the New Haven Colony.

THE PEQUOT WAR

As many as 30,000 Native Americans lived in Connecticut when the Europeans first arrived. Soon European diseases, such as smallpox and scarlet fever, spread among the Native people, killing thousands. Colonists meanwhile claimed more and more of their land. The Pequots in eastern Connecticut struck back. Pequot warriors kept the English fort at Saybrook under constant attack in late 1636.

In May 1637, Captain John Mason raised an army of 90 settlers. These armed men were joined by about 70 Mohegan and 200 Narragansett warriors. They marched against the Pequot fort at Mystic. In a night attack, they surrounded the fort and set it on fire. Pequots who tried to escape were shot. As many as 700 Pequots, including women and children, were killed in the massacre. Many Pequot survivors were enslaved and sent to English colonies in the Caribbean. After

Picture Yourself . . .

Traveling through the Wilderness
Stories of Connecticut's rich farmland have attracted you and about 100 men, women, and children—led by Reverend Thomas Hooker—to set out from Newtown (now Cambridge), Massachusetts. It is June 1636, and your group—along with a herd of 160 cows, goats, and pigs—will make the 100-mile (160 km) journey to Hartford through the wilderness. You have no one to guide you, only a compass to help you find your way. With a pack on your back that holds everything you own—clothes, tools, weapons, pots, and pans—you climb over mountains, swim across rivers, wade through swamps, and cut swaths through thick woods on the way. Exhausted at the end of each day, you still have to milk the cows and cook your dinner. Finally, you can rest, lying on the ground and gazing at the stars overhead.

Reverend Thomas Hooker and his congregation stop to rest during their journey to Connecticut.

another battle in 1637 at Fairfield Swamp, the defeated Pequots were unable to resist the colonists.

The numbers of several of the Algonquian groups in the region dwindled as Algonquian peoples struggled to survive the threats of disease and attack. And many of the more than 20 Algonquian groups found in the area upon European arrival united together to survive.

DEMOCRATIC GOVERNMENT

The Puritans who first settled in Connecticut established a theocracy, a community governed by its religious leaders. When Reverend Thomas Hooker arrived in Hartford, he brought new ideas to the colony. He believed the colonists had the right to play a larger role in their government. In a sermon he delivered in May 1638, Hooker insisted, "The choice of public magistrates [judges] belongs unto the people. . . . The privilege of election . . . belongs to the people."

The towns of the Connecticut Colony designed the Fundamental Orders in 1639. These 11 orders established a new colonial government. Its general court could make laws, collect taxes, grant public lands to people and towns, and perform other duties. Only adult men who owned property could vote. The Fundamental Orders are considered the first written **constitution** in the Americas. Today, one of Connecticut's nicknames is the Constitution State.

In 1661, Connecticut settlers began to worry that their new English king, Charles II, might not accept their democratic form of government, so their governor, John Winthrop, sailed for England.

WORD TO KNOW

constitution *a set of laws organizing a government*

Puritan Reverend John Davenport preaches to his followers on their first Sunday at Quinnipiac.

On May 10, 1662, Winthrop finally convinced the king to grant Connecticut an official charter. This legal document allowed the colony many freedoms. Connecticut voters could select their governor, judges, and assemblymen. At first, the people of the New Haven Colony wanted a separate charter because they did not want to become part of Connecticut. But in 1664, they reached a compromise, and on January 5, 1665, the New Haven Colony became part of the Connecticut Colony.

In October 1687, Sir Edmund Andros, royal governor of New England, rode into Hartford demanding that the Connecticut Charter be turned over to him. Andros wanted the governor and assemblymen to recognize him as its rightful ruler. According to legend, assemblymen blew out the candles that lit the meeting room. In the dark, Captain Joseph Wadsworth ran off with the document and hid it in the hollow of a great oak tree. Andros really was in control of the colony, but he had been ignoring Connecticut's new government. He believed New York and Massachusetts were more important parts of his responsibilities as royal governor. Andros returned to Boston, where he remained until citizens there arrested him in 1689.

The oak tree where the document was hidden came to be known as the Charter Oak.

LIFE IN COLONIAL CONNECTICUT

"One for the bug, one for the crow, one to rot, and one to grow." This was a rhyme Connecticut's farmers often repeated about planting four kernels of corn. Farming was hard in the 1700s. Every member of the

Farmers harvesting pumpkins

YANKEE PEDDLERS

Yankee peddlers sold goods to Connecticut's farmers. These salesmen would arrive on wagons bursting with pots, pans, brooms, baskets, buttons, ribbons, pins, nails, and lots of other products. Yankee peddlers were also known as "nutmeg men." They sold nutmegs, large seeds that smell good and are used to flavor foods. Today, one of Connecticut's nicknames is the Nutmeg State.

family had to work. Boys helped clear fields. Farmers dug up stones to pile at the edges of their fields. Stone walls kept cattle either in their pastures or out of the crops. Boys chopped wood and stacked the pieces into piles. Families needed firewood for cooking and heat. It took the trees of 0.6 acres (.24 ha) of land to heat one small house each winter. Of course, the plow horse, cows, pigs, and chickens all needed to be tended and fed. Boys did that, and sometimes girls did these chores, too. But usually girls worked inside the house. Cooking, washing, sewing, and looking after younger siblings kept girls busy most of the time. Boys and girls also had to go to the well and get buckets of water several times a day.

Connecticut farmers grew many of the same crops the Algonquian peoples did, such as corn, beans, squash, and pumpkins. They also planted grains such as wheat and rye. Farmers around Wethersfield harvested onions. Near Windsor, tobacco became a valuable crop. Along the coast, salt grass grew naturally in the marshes, and farmers fed it to their cattle in wintertime.

The typical colonial town in Connecticut consisted of a single road with a few homes and shops on each side. Some towns had a tavern or an inn. Connecticut's Puritan farmers rode into town every Sunday to worship at the meetinghouse. As towns grew, the people built Congregational churches. Painted white, topped with high towers called steeples, these churches are still easy to find in Connecticut today.

A 1650 law insisted that towns of 50 or more families hire a teacher. The teacher carried a stick, which he used to hit pupils who misbehaved. He listened as children read aloud and watched as they wrote their lessons. Some young men went to college. Yale College was founded in 1701 in Killingworth and moved to New Haven in 1717. Yale is the third-oldest college in the United States.

AFRICAN AMERICANS IN COLONIAL CONNECTICUT

At the end of the 17th century, slavery had become legal in Connecticut and other New England colonies. New London was a bustling port for trade, including slave labor. People of color were advertised for sale in Connecticut newspapers and sold at auction at other port cities in Connecticut.

Africans were part of a slave system that included Native Americans, the first people enslaved in the Americas. By 1750, more than 3,000 people of African descent lived in Connecticut, about 3 percent of the population—constituting the largest black population in New England.

Read all about it! The first issue of the *Connecticut Courant* was published in 1764. Later, the newspaper changed its name to the *Hartford Courant*. It is the oldest continuously operating newspaper in the United States!

WORDS TO KNOW

bondage *a state of being held against one's will*

militiamen *members of a group of citizens organized for military duty*

Connecticut's enslaved people worked as clerks, farmers, mechanics, cooks, and servants, among other occupations. Many black men served in Connecticut's whaling industry, where they traveled and had much more independence than most other enslaved people.

Enslaved Indians and Africans sometimes escaped **bondage** and fought against those who enforced it. In 1660, a night raid by Africans and Indians terrified white residents of Hartford. Thirty years later, three men—one African, one Indian, and one English—were arrested in Newbury, Massachusetts, for plotting with the French to overthrow British colonial rule.

REVOLUTIONARY YEARS

During the French and Indian War (1756–1763), some 5,000 Connecticut men marched off to fight in New York and Canada. Later, to help pay for the war between France and England, the British Parliament taxed the American colonies. The 1765 Stamp Act taxed paper items including newspapers, legal documents, advertisements, and even playing cards. To protest the tax, some Connecticut men formed a group called the Sons of Liberty.

In September 1765, 500 members of the Sons surrounded Jared Ingersoll and forced him to resign as Connecticut's tax collector. Protests in other colonies forced the British Parliament to do away with the Stamp Act in 1766. The 1767 Townshend Acts, however, taxed goods imported into the colonies such as glass, paint, lead, cloth, wine, and tea. In 1773, Massachusetts protesters tossed chests of tea into Boston Harbor in what was known as the Boston Tea Party. Then, in April 1775, Massachusetts **militiamen** battled British troops at Lexington and Concord. The American Revolution had begun.

Nearly 32,000 Connecticut men joined the Continental army to fight for independence. In 1775, Connecticut general Israel Putnam commanded troops at the Battle of Bunker Hill in Massachusetts. Born in Connecticut's Litchfield County, Ethan Allen led his "Green Mountain Boys" to capture Fort Ticonderoga in New York. Enslaved men were recruited to fight for American independence, and Connecticut had a black company. About 5,000 people of African descent enlisted in the successful fight to drive the British from North America. Lemuel Haynes, born in West Hartford to an African father and a white mother, was an indentured servant until he was 21. Then, as a **minuteman**, he helped the Green Mountain Boys capture Fort Ticonderoga.

WORD TO KNOW

minuteman *a member of a group who would fight at a minute's notice during the American Revolution*

Townspeople gather outside a recruiting office in New London during the Revolutionary War.

Benedict Arnold, Hero or Villain?

Born in Norwich, Benedict Arnold (1741–1801) fought in many battles and rose to the rank of major general. At the Battle of Saratoga in October 1777, his leadership helped the Americans win an important victory. By 1780, however, he had decided to betray the American cause. He planned to surrender the American fort at West Point, New York, to the British. His plot was foiled before he could carry it out. But he escaped capture. Arnold spent the rest of the war fighting for the British. Was Arnold a hero or a villain?

HERO

"Nothing could exceed the bravery of Arnold on this day. . . . There seemed to shoot out from him a magnetic flame that electrified his men and made heroes of all within his influence."—American captain Ebenezer Wakefield, recalling the Battle of Saratoga

VILLAIN

"Honor and virtue were strangers to his soul. He was naturally a coward and never went in the way of danger."—American major general Anthony Wayne, after the discovery of the West Point plot

In 1776, East Haddam schoolteacher Nathan Hale was captured and sentenced to hang by the British for spying in New York. It is said Hale's last words were: "I regret that I have but one life to lose for my country."

British soldiers marched into Connecticut several times during the war. In April 1777, British troops headed to Danbury to burn Continental army supplies. But a 16-year-old woman named Sybil Ludington, from just across the border in New York, rode more than 40 miles (64 km) to warn her father's soldiers of the British advancement. Sometimes called the female Paul Revere, she rode twice as far as the Massachusetts patriot did.

The British returned in February 1779 and damaged

In 1775 in Old Saybrook, David Bushnell built the world's first submarine to be used in battle. The one-person underwater boat, made of wood and metal, was named the *Turtle*.

the town of Greenwich before General Putnam's militiamen forced them to retreat. In July 1779, 3,000 British soldiers struck at New Haven, Fairfield, and Norwalk, torching houses, barns, shops, mills, and churches. In September 1781, 2,000 British troops led by Connecticut-born Benedict Arnold attacked Fort Trumbull and Fort Griswold at the mouth of the Thames River. Fort Trumbull soon fell into British hands. But the 150 men of Fort Griswold fought back, killing many of the enemy. But the British finally captured that fort, too.

Connecticut provided the war effort with food and supplies. Mills in East Hartford, Windham, New Haven, Stratford, Glastonbury, and Salisbury manufactured gunpowder. Gunsmiths in Mansfield, Windham, and Goshen provided Connecticut soldiers with muskets and pistols. At coastal forts, cannons and cannonballs produced at the Salisbury foundry defended against enemy attack. A ship built in Connecticut, the *Oliver Cromwell*, captured 13 British ships during the war.

The Revolutionary War ended in 1783. The people of Connecticut, led by Governor Jonathan Trumbull, certainly had done their part to help win independence. Is it any surprise that today one of Connecticut's nicknames is the **Provision** State?

SEE IT HERE!

OLD NEW-GATE PRISON AND COPPER MINE

Deep, damp, and dark. In East Granby, miners began digging America's first chartered copper mine in 1707. From 1773 to 1827, the mine was used as a colonial and state prison called Old New-Gate. During the Revolutionary War, British prisoners sat in the chilly tunnels 50 feet (15 m) below the ground. You can still climb down into the prison today.

WORD TO KNOW

provision *the act of providing, or a supply of needed materials*

A woman is stopped from shooting Benedict Arnold following the British attack on New London in 1781.

42

READ ABOUT

In 1787, George Washington led the Constitutional Convention in Philadelphia.

1788

Connecticut becomes the fifth state to ratify the Constitution

1793 ▲

Eli Whitney invents the cotton gin

1814

Eli Terry designs a popular shelf clock

CHAPTER FOUR

GROWTH AND CHANGE

★

S OLDIERS MARCHED HOME AND PUT AWAY THEIR GUNS. Sailors sailed into peaceful harbors and anchored their ships. In the 1783 Treaty of Paris, Great Britain finally recognized the United States as a free and independent nation. Delegates gathered in Philadelphia in 1787 to write a national constitution.

1852 ▲

Harriet Beecher Stowe writes Uncle Tom's Cabin

1861–1865

Connecticut citizens support the Union during the Civil War

1900

About one-quarter of the state's population is foreign-born.

WORD TO KNOW

convention *a group of people meeting for a common purpose*

Connecticut: From Colony to Statehood (1636–1788)

This map shows the original Connecticut territory (outlined in green) and the area that became the state of Connecticut in 1788.

ROGER SHERMAN AND THE CONSTITUTION

Roger Sherman was one of Connecticut's delegates to the Constitutional **Convention**. John Adams described Sherman as "that old Puritan, honest as an angel." It was Sherman who solved a big problem at the convention. How would the states be represented in the new national government? Small states wanted all of the states to be represented equally. Larger states wanted all representatives elected in proportion to their populations. Finally, Sherman suggested that Congress should be divided into

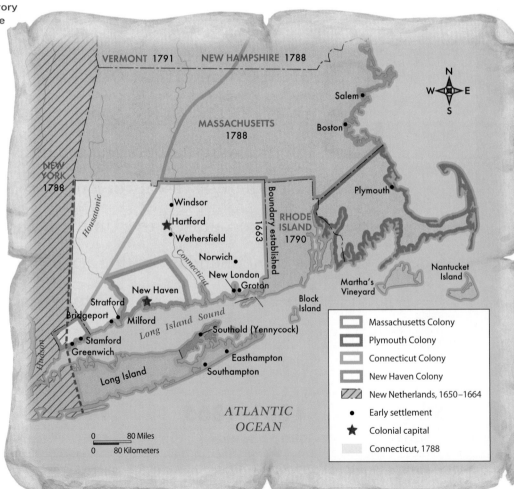

Massachusetts Colony
Plymouth Colony
Connecticut Colony
New Haven Colony
New Netherlands, 1650–1664
• Early settlement
★ Colonial capital
Connecticut, 1788

two branches. In the House of Representatives, members of Congress would be elected according to a state's population. In the Senate, however, there would be an equal number of senators (two) from each state. In the end, Sherman's "Connecticut Compromise" was agreed to. Of the 13 original states, on January 9, 1788, Connecticut became the fifth to **ratify** the United States Constitution.

WORD TO KNOW

ratify *approve officially*

NUTMEGGERS ON THE MOVE

These days, most Americans move at least once—maybe from an apartment to a house or from one town to another. In the 1800s, many people in Connecticut began calling themselves Nutmeggers because they moved from place to place as often as the Yankee peddlers who sold nutmegs. Why were they moving so much? With too many people and not enough land, thousands of families packed up and left Connecticut.

Before 1800, many of these families resettled in Vermont and New York. As the years passed, others headed farther west. The federal government granted Connecticut settlers land in the region called the Western Reserve

Roger Sherman (center) meets with Thomas Jefferson (left) and Benjamin Franklin.

MINI-BIO

NOAH WEBSTER: THE DICTIONARY MAN

In the 1700s, many Americans could read and write. But they did not always agree on spelling. It was Noah Webster (1758–1843) who solved that problem. Born in West Hartford, Webster attended Yale College and became a schoolteacher. He believed all Americans should spell words the same way and understand their meanings. In 1806, he published his first dictionary. It was a great success. He continued to add words and definitions in later editions. They included words that were especially American, such as "squash" and "skunk." When he finished his work, Webster's dictionary contained 70,000 words. Today, *Webster's Third New International Dictionary, Unabridged* has more than 476,000 entries.

? **Want to know more?** Visit www.factsfornow .scholastic.com and enter the keyword **Connecticut**.

under the Articles of Confederation. Moses Cleaveland of Canterbury, Connecticut, settled along the Ohio shore of Lake Erie. His settlement grew into the busy city of Cleveland. Connecticut settlers established themselves in Indiana, Illinois, Michigan, Wisconsin, Minnesota, and later, Kansas. These settlers took part in their new state governments. Alexis de Tocqueville, a French visitor, noted in 1832 that one-third of all U.S. senators and one-quarter of U.S. representatives had been born in Connecticut!

GETTING AROUND

The Farmington Canal, completed in 1840, carried farm crops, factory goods, and passengers between New Haven and Northampton, Massachusetts. The entire 70-mile (113-km) trip could be completed in two days. The canal closed in 1848, the year trains began running from New Haven to New York City. They belched smoke and roared along their iron tracks at speeds reaching 30 miles per hour (48 kph). The Central Valley Railroad started operating in 1871 along the Connecticut River.

Shipping and shipbuilding were important Connecticut industries for many years. There were busy shipyards in Essex, Lyme, Deep River, Chester, and East Haddam, where skilled workers built hundreds of sailing ships, fishing ships, and whaling ships during the 1800s. The state's first steamboat, the *Experiment*, began making regular trips between Hartford and Essex in 1822. For boat safety, a system of lights began operating along the Connecticut River in 1856.

THE CAMPAIGN TO END SLAVERY

In 1793, Connecticut schoolteacher Eli Whitney visited a Georgia cotton **plantation**. Hearing that it was difficult to separate cottonseeds from the soft white cotton fiber, Whitney invented a machine that did the job easily. His cotton gin (short for engine) made cotton a more valuable crop, but that in turn created a demand for a larger labor force, which plantation owners filled with slave labor. In the years that followed, ships brought thousands of kidnapped Africans to the United States to work as slaves on Southern plantations. The Southern planters grew dependent on slavery to support the region's economy.

WORD TO KNOW

plantation *an estate or farm where crops are planted*

Enslaved laborers in the South use Eli Whitney's cotton gin.

FREEDOM FIGHTER

At age 20, James W. Pennington (1807–1870) escaped from slavery in Maryland. He was taught to read, write, and master arithmetic and geography by a white Quaker in Philadelphia, Pennsylvania. He moved to New Haven to study for the ministry at Yale. He was not admitted to the school but was allowed to sit in on classes. In 1838, he was licensed to preach, and he became president of the Hartford Central Association of Congregational Ministers. He was chosen as a delegate in 1843 to the World's Anti-Slavery Convention and the World Peace Convention in London.

Pennington wrote the first textbook history of African American people, and he led civil rights demonstrations in New York in 1855 and 1856 that eventually desegregated its horse-drawn streetcar lines.

Before the end of the Revolutionary War, Northern states had moved to end slavery. New England states, with their short growing season, were not dependent on slave labor for their prosperity and were the first to end the practice. Businesspeople in the North wanted a free labor force they could hire and fire and would not have to care for year-round. Abolitionist societies formed by whites and free African Americans also prodded residents of Northern states to live up to the Revolutionary promise of liberty.

In 1784, the Connecticut Assembly passed a gradual emancipation law that freed its slaves when they reached the age of 25. The freed people were not granted equal rights until many years later. Connecticut's 1818 constitutional convention restricted voting rights to white adult men. In 1848, a state law ended slavery completely in Connecticut. Even so, African Americans did not gain full citizenship rights until after the Civil War—in 1870.

THE UNDERGROUND RAILROAD

In the Northern states, slavery was not profitable. Many Northerners also believed slavery was cruel and evil.

During the 1830s and 1840s, an antislavery movement called abolition spread. Abolitionists demanded an end to slavery. Both black and white abolitionists developed a secret escape system called the Underground Railroad. Runaway slaves followed the routes to freedom in the North and Canada. People in Connecticut towns such as Deep River, Hartford, Killingly, Middletown, and Willimantic offered rest stops for some of these runaway slaves. In fact, Farmington became the "Grand Central Station" of Connecticut's Underground Railroad lines.

Townspeople in Canterbury set fire to Prudence Crandall's school.

PRUDENCE CRANDALL: FIGHTING FOR FAIRNESS

Prudence Crandall (1803–1890) opened a private school for girls in 1831 in Canterbury. Although only white girls attended, she saw no reason why 19-year-old African American Sarah Harris should not be admitted as a student. But outraged parents of white students removed their daughters from classes. Then Crandall opened her school for black girls only. A mob smashed the school's windows with rocks. Crandall was arrested and spent a night in jail. For the safety of her students, she closed her school. But her bravery and fairness are remembered today. Along with Nathan Hale, Prudence Crandall is one of Connecticut's official state heroes.

? **Want to know more?** Visit www.factsfornow .scholastic.com and enter the keyword **Connecticut**.

African American pastor Amos Beman helped many runaways on the Underground Railroad. He paid this tribute to them:

Those who come with fear and trembling and apply for aid, are flying from the cruel prison house—the dark land of their unpaid toil—the ground stained with their blood and wet with their bitter tears . . . they have journeyed with scant food, guided by the pale light of the North Star . . . the somber light has been their day . . . the cold damp earth their cheerless bed . . . the dreary day has been full of danger and alarm . . . every stirring leap spoke to them of the slave-hunter . . . every sound told them of the bloodhound.

In 1852, Litchfield-born writer Harriet Beecher Stowe published a novel called *Uncle Tom's Cabin*. It told about the horrors of slave life and sold 3 million copies in just a few years. More than ever, Northerners were persuaded that slavery had to be abolished.

THE *AMISTAD* SLAVE REVOLT

In the spring of 1839, slave traders in West Africa raided villages where people of the Mendi culture lived and captured dozens of them. Mendi men, women, and children were shipped in chains across the Atlantic Ocean. On the island of Cuba, they were sold into slavery. Some of these

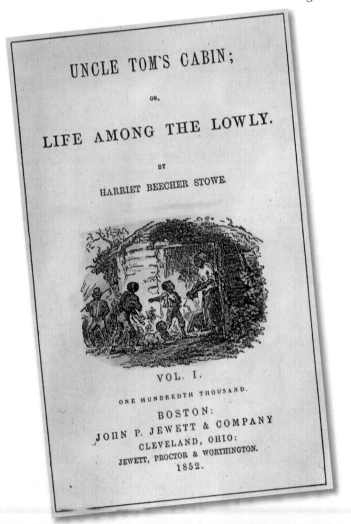

The title page from the first edition of *Uncle Tom's Cabin*

Mendi were herded aboard a Spanish schooner, the *Amistad*, for shipment to America. The Mendi, led by Sengbe Pieh (later known as Joseph Cinque), rose in revolt. After a fight with the crew, the Mendi seized control of the ship and tried to sail to Africa. However, they were not successful. The ship finally drifted into Long Island Sound and was brought into the harbor at New London, Connecticut.

Were these Africans free or slaves? The Mendi were jailed in New Haven for months while the courts decided their case. Connecticut citizens gave money and hired lawyers to help them. In the end, former president John Quincy Adams successfully argued their case before the U.S. Supreme Court. For the next nine months, the Mendi were free, living in Farmington, Connecticut. By November 1841, abolitionists raised the money to pay for their voyage home. Thirty-seven known survivors of the *Amistad* revolt reached Africa in January 1842.

The Mendi were freed after the U.S. Supreme Court ruled in their favor.

MRS. STOWE VISITS WASHINGTON

When Harriet Beecher Stowe, author of the best-selling *Uncle Tom's Cabin*, visited the White House during the Civil War, it is said that President Lincoln greeted her with, "So you're the little woman who wrote that book that started this great war."

FAQ

Q8 WHAT ARE SOME OF THE THINGS FIRST MADE IN CONNECTICUT?

A8

1818 First mass-produced chairs (Lambert Hitchcock, Riverton)

1820 American plows (at Wethersfield)

1830 American hoopskirts (at Derby)

1834 American friction matches (Thomas Sanford, Beacon Falls)

1856 Canned milk (Gail Borden, Torrington)

1877 American bicycles (Hartford)

1895 Mechanical player-piano (H. K. Wilcox, Meriden)

1899 Football tackling dummy (Alonzo Stagg, Yale University)

THE CIVIL WAR

Southern slaveholders feared that President Abraham Lincoln and the U.S. Congress would halt the spread of slavery. By the spring of 1861, 11 Southern states declared their independence from the United States and formed the Confederate States of America. They fired on the U.S. base at Fort Sumter, South Carolina, and Lincoln called for volunteer troops. He wanted them to put down the Southern rebellion and preserve the Union. Within three days of Lincoln's call, Connecticut men formed the state's first volunteer army regiment. By the end of the war, 55,000 Connecticut troops had served in the Union army or navy. Of this number, about 20,000 were killed or wounded. Connecticut soldiers fought in dozens of major battles. These included the bloody battles of Antietam, Fredericksburg, Chancellorsville, Gettysburg, and Vicksburg.

So many African American men from Connecticut rushed to serve in the Union army during the Civil War that they filled two full regiments. One in every four Union sailors was an African American.

Connecticut's citizens did all they could to support their troops. People collected blankets, clothing, medicines, and food to send to the soldiers. Connecticut factories manufactured thousands of muskets, rifles, pistols, knives, and other weapons. The Ames Iron Works in Falls Village built cannons. The Hazard Powder Company in Enfield made a staggering 12 tons of gunpowder each day! Other factories produced uniforms, boots, blankets, rubber rain covers, saddles, and wagons. In 1865, the Civil War ended with Northern victory. The Union was preserved and slavery abolished. Connecticut's troops came marching home.

In an 1853 painting by John Whetten Ehninger, a Yankee peddler displays some of his wares.

MADE IN CONNECTICUT

At his factory in Plymouth, Connecticut, Eli Terry made clocks. By 1814, he had designed a shelf clock that could be manufactured quickly and cheaply. Seth Thomas and other Connecticut clockmakers followed his example. Soon Yankee peddlers were selling Connecticut clocks all over the country. In 1844, an English traveler reported, "Wherever we have been, in Kentucky, in Indiana, in Illinois, in Missouri, . . . in cabins where there was not a chair to sit on, there was sure to be a Connecticut clock."

After Eli Whitney invented the cotton gin, cotton mills sprang up in Manchester, Vernon, Pomfret, and other Connecticut towns. Thousands of mill machine workers produced cotton thread and cloth. In 1798, Whitney established a gun factory in Hamden, where he designed a system to mass-produce guns. Other manufacturers soon began using Whitney's "American

Thomaston was named for clockmaker Seth Thomas.

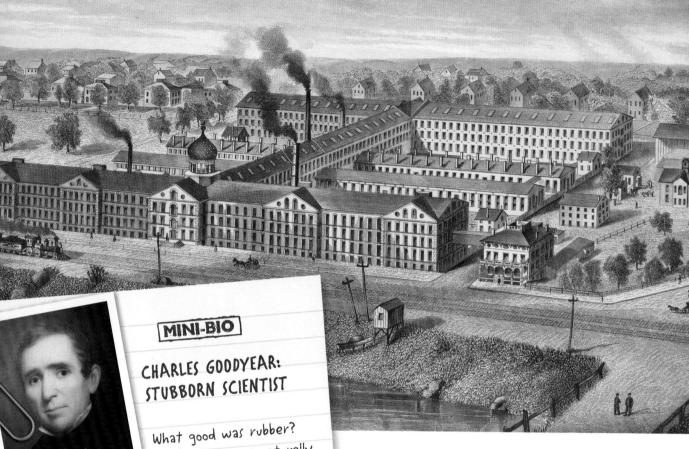

Colt's factory in Hartford in the mid-19th century

MINI-BIO

CHARLES GOODYEAR: STUBBORN SCIENTIST

What good was rubber? Raw rubber was naturally waterproof—and it could be formed into raincoats and boots—but it couldn't survive hot or cold weather. In the heat, it melted, and in the cold, it cracked. Born in New Haven, Charles Goodyear (1800–1860) set out to solve the problem. At last in 1839, he discovered the solution by accident when a mix of rubber and sulfur fell onto his hot stove. Goodyear scraped it off and realized it had become a dry, stretchable material. The word he used to describe the process that made rubber usable is "vulcanization."

? **Want to know more?** Visit www.factsfornow .scholastic.com and enter the keyword **Connecticut**.

system" of mass production. Samuel Colt built the world's largest gun factory in Hartford in 1855. Colt's workers were making 1,000 guns each day by 1857. A visitor at the factory declared, "Each portion of the firearm [gun or other weapon] has its particular section. . . . The first group of machines appears to be employed in chambering the cylinders; here another is boring barrels; another group is milling the lock frames; still another is drilling them." The days of one craftsperson building a gun from start to finish were over.

NEW WORKERS

In the 1840s, a disease struck potato crops in Ireland, leading to widespread starvation in what became known as the Potato Famine. Thousands of Irish immigrants, desperate for work, sailed to America and settled in Connecticut. They helped build roads and worked in factories. Before and after the Civil War, thousands of other foreigners, mostly from Europe, crossed the ocean and settled in Connecticut. By 1900, about 225,000 of the state's population of 908,000 had been born in a foreign country. Most were from Ireland, Germany, Canada, England, and Italy. They proudly added their strength and determination to Connecticut's workforce.

Irish immigrants aboard a ship bound for the United States in 1850

READ ABOUT

The Colt factory in Hartford supplied the U.S. military with pistols while the country was engaged in World War I.

1920s

More than one quarter of the state's textile mills close

1930

Democrat Wilbur Cross is elected governor during the Depression

▲ **1941–1945**

State aircraft and boat industries help win World War II

CHAPTER FIVE

MORE MODERN TIMES

★

W HEN THE UNITED STATES ENTERED WORLD WAR I IN 1917, THOUSANDS OF CONNECTICUT MEN JOINED THE ARMY. Many served on the battlefields of France. At home, Connecticut's women worked in factories, which manufactured trainload after trainload of military supplies. By the end of the war in 1918, 80 percent of Connecticut's factories were producing weapons and war materials.

◄**1960s**

Hartford is recognized as the insurance capital of the world

◄**1981**

Thirman Milner becomes mayor and starts work to revitalize Hartford

2012

Hurricane Sandy slams into Connecticut

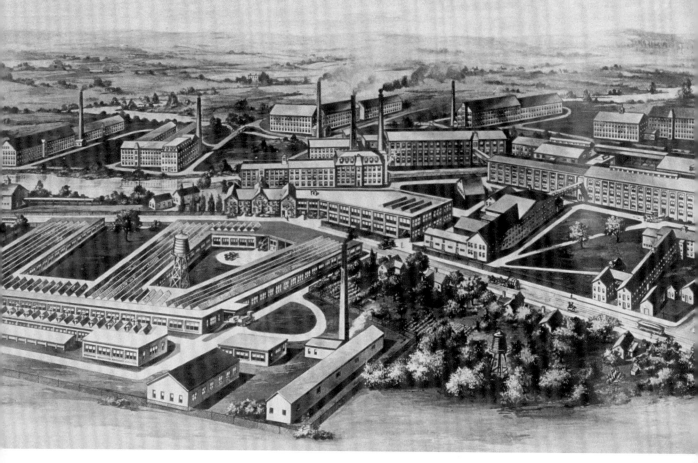

Connecticut was home to many factories, including the Russell Manufacturing Company, which produced textiles in a large facility in Middletown.

THE ROARING TWENTIES

The end of the war was not all good for Connecticut workers. Factories that made war materials suddenly closed, and thousands of workers lost their jobs. Troops returning home from Europe joined growing unemployment lines. Could things get worse? Unfortunately, yes. Of the state's 47 textile mills, 14 closed in the 1920s. It was cheaper to manufacture cloth in the Southern states. Connecticut looked for new ways to employ its workforce.

Meanwhile, Americans wanted automobiles and new electric products such as refrigerators. Connecticut factory workers began making electric cable, switches, light sockets, and motors. Five factories in Bridgeport turned out automobile parts, such as gearshifts and brake linings. The Pratt & Whitney Aircraft Company in Hartford started producing air-cooled airplane engines in 1925. As the economy improved, people in Connecticut began enjoying the roaring, carefree lifestyle of the 1920s.

THE GREAT DEPRESSION

Following a stock market crash in October 1929, the United States plunged more deeply into what became known as the Great Depression. Many Connecticut workers found themselves jobless. By 1932, about 150,000 Connecticut workers were unemployed.

Since 1915, the Republicans, led by politician J. Henry Roraback, had controlled the state government. In 1930, Democrat Wilbur Cross of Mansfield ran for governor, declaring that "the Republican organization and its leaders have been settin' on rotten eggs for fifteen years without hatching any chickens." Cross was elected, and he remained governor until 1939. During the Depression, he looked for ways to provide Connecticut citizens with financial relief and steady work.

In 1934, the state government spent $29 million on work projects for 40,000 people. Across the state, new roads, bridges, and sewers were built. Governor Cross took advantage of federal programs offered by President Franklin Roosevelt's New Deal, such as the Works Progress Administration (WPA). The WPA employed thousands of people to repair state hospitals, prisons, police barracks, and college dormitories, among other projects. The New Deal's Civilian Conservation Corps (CCC) put 15,000 young men to work in Connecticut. They cut brush and built roads in state and national parks.

SEE IT HERE!

GILLETTE CASTLE

William Gillette (1855–1937) became a rich and famous actor. For years, he played the role of detective Sherlock Holmes onstage. In East Haddam, you can see the unique mansion he built in 1919. Perched above the Connecticut River, the gray stone house looks like a giant sand castle. Inside, there are secret mirrors, hidden rooms and passageways, and a room furnished to look like Sherlock Holmes's study. Outside, Gillette ran a small-sized railroad around his estate. Today, the grounds are a beautiful state park.

Women inspect pistol parts at a plant in Hartford in the 1940s.

MINI-BIO

LEMUEL R. CUSTIS: A TUSKEGEE AIRMAN

Captain Lemuel R. Custis (1915–2005), of Hartford, learned how to fly a fighter plane at the Tuskegee Institute in Alabama. During World War II, he flew combat missions with the famous all-black 99th Fighter Squadron over Europe. On January 27, 1944, Captain Custis spotted a German FW190 fighter plane. He zoomed ahead with the machine guns of his P-40 fighter blazing and shot the enemy aircraft out of the sky!

Want to know more? Visit www.factsfornow .scholastic.com and enter the keyword **Connecticut**.

WORLD WAR II

It took another war to end the Great Depression in the United States. When Japan attacked the American naval base at Pearl Harbor, Hawai'i, on December 7, 1941, the United States entered the war against Japan, Germany, and Italy. Connecticut governor Raymond Baldwin had earlier exclaimed that American liberty "cannot be purchased with goods and gold; we must sacrifice blood to preserve freedom." Many Connecticut men and women served in the armed forces. Factory employment in the state quickly rose from 350,000 in 1939 to 550,000 by the end of 1944—and 35,000 of these new workers were women. Thousands of African Americans traveled from the South to jobs in the North. Many Connecticut factories produced weapons, and others made airplane engines and even entire fighter planes. The Electric Boat Company in Groton made 75 submarines for the U.S. Navy during the war.

World War II ended in 1945 with the defeat of Germany and with Japan's surrender. By that time, the U.S. government had ordered $8 billion in weapons, ammunition, aircraft, ships, and other war materials from Connecticut!

FROM YESTERDAY TO TODAY

After World War II, Connecticut continued to grow and change. Woods and farmland slowly gave way to suburban development. The cities of Hartford, New Haven, and Bridgeport all lost people. Towns outside these cities, however, mushroomed in size. The populations of Bloomfield, just north of Hartford, as well as Orange

Cornwall's Mohawk Ski Area was the first ski resort in the United States to make artificial snow, in 1948.

In the 1960s, the Connecticut countryside was perfect for leisure and vacation spots.

In 1954, David N. Mullaney of Fairfield invented a plastic ball with holes in it. He called it the Wiffle ball! Still a Connecticut institution, Wiffle balls are manufactured in Shelton.

WORD TO KNOW

optics *lenses, prisms, or mirrors used to aid one in seeing; found, for example, in glasses, microscopes, and telescopes*

and Trumbull farther south, more than doubled in size between 1950 and 1960. Many residents of Connecticut's Fairfield County commuted from their suburban homes to work in New York City just over the border.

What kind of work kept laborers in Connecticut busy? Making aircraft engines and other plane parts still employed thousands after World War II. Danbury had been famous for hat making since Zadoc Benedict started the first hat factory in the United States there in 1780. By 1949, 66 percent of all the hats made in America came from Connecticut! Back then, everybody wore hats all the time. But hats went out of fashion in the 1960s. Danbury workers then found jobs in growing **optics** and electronics factories. During that decade, Hartford became known as the home of the insurance industry. Insurance companies such as the Hartford, the Travelers, and Aetna employed thousands.

While Connecticut's rising middle class moved from cities to the suburbs, its economically disadvantaged people were left behind, unable to afford to buy houses there. They were stuck, and the cities began to suffer from the loss of revenue. In the 1950s, buildings fell into ruin, schools decayed, and crime began to rise. In New Haven, Richard Lee, the mayor from 1953 to 1970, tried to help. He persuaded the federal government to invest $110 million in rebuilding New Haven. Construction workers built new high-rise apartment and office buildings, and the Chapel Square Mall attracted shoppers back downtown. Other Connecticut cities tried to follow New Haven's example. In downtown Hartford, Constitution Plaza opened in 1962.

While the state government tried to improve the lives of all its citizens, disadvantaged blacks, living in what was called the inner city, often felt they were forgotten.

In the summer of 1967, riots erupted in Bridgeport, Hartford, Middletown, New Britain, New Haven, New London, Norwalk, Stamford, and Waterbury. In April 1968, civil rights leader Martin Luther King Jr. was assassinated, sparking more rioting in Connecticut's cities. In Hartford, rioters set the public library on fire and damaged 100 buildings. It took soldiers of the National Guard to bring calm to New Haven. Connecticut's African American population demanded fair treatment. The state's Latino communities also began raising their voices. Between 1960 and 1970, more than 80,000 Spanish-speaking people moved to Connecticut's cities.

Flamenco dancers perform at Puerto Rican Day in Bridgeport.

MINI-BIO

THIRMAN MILNER: HARTFORD MAYOR

By 1980, Hartford's population was 34 percent African American. Racial tensions gripped the city. Some black citizens demanded their fair share of police and fire protection, street repairs, and health care centers. In 1981, State Representative Thirman Milner (1934—) ran for mayor. "We're going to have a citywide love-in," he promised. Voters elected him by a wide margin, and he became the first African American mayor of a New England city. During his six years as mayor, Milner helped improve life in Hartford and lift the spirits of its people.

? **Want to know more?** Visit www.factsfornow.scholastic.com and enter the keyword **Connecticut.**

64

MINI-BIO

CARRIE SAXON PERRY: A HISTORIC JOURNEY

Carrie Saxon Perry (1931–) had already served seven years in Connecticut's House of Representatives when she decided to run for mayor of Hartford in 1987. As a black woman, she hoped to be a good role model for the young. In a speech, she declared, "I . . . want young people to believe in government and believe that those who want to, can serve!" Perry won the election. She became the first African American woman elected mayor of a major city in the Northeast.

? Want to know more? Visit www.factsfornow .scholastic.com and enter the keyword **Connecticut**.

In 1969, the U.S. Justice Department ordered an end to school segregation in Waterbury. It was the first of many New England cities ordered to do so. Before long, school buses throughout Connecticut carried inner-city students to better funded suburban schools. Blacks and Hispanics continued to gain opportunities in education and employment throughout the 1980s and 1990s.

Cheerleaders from Wilby High School in Waterbury pose during a football game. Waterbury's schools were integrated in 1969.

Hartford skyline

The economy, too, continued to remain strong in Connecticut into the 21st century, in large part because of the strong defense industry. The U.S. Defense Department spends approximately twice the national average per person in the state. In 2002, $6.2 billion went to defense industry–related contracts in Connecticut.

Connecticut prides itself on the progress it has made since the 1600s. Hartford's tall, gleaming skyscrapers remind us how modern a city it has become. Yet the Constitution State has not forgotten its past. It continues to offer a look back in time at places such as Mystic Seaport and dozens of small towns and villages that have retained their old-time charm. Connecticut keeps its eye on the future, confident that its best years are still to come!

READ ABOUT

Fans celebrate after the University of Connecticut women's basketball team won the NCAA championship in 2013.

CHAPTER SIX

PEPLE

★

CONNECTICUT IS A SMALL STATE WITH A LONG AND COLORFUL HISTORY. People have come from every spot on the globe to settle in the Nutmeg State, bringing their unique cultural traditions with them. Whether they live in cities, suburbs, or rural areas, it is Connecticut's people, with their diverse backgrounds, who make the state come alive.

Big City Life

This list shows the population of Connecticut's biggest cities.

Bridgeport 144,355
New Haven 129,946
Hartford. 124,744
Stamford 122,643
Waterbury 110,366
Norwalk 85,653

Source: U.S. Census Bureau, 2010 census

WHO LIVES IN CONNECTICUT?

Connecticut may be the third-smallest state, but it packs a lot of punch! Its population of more than 3.6 million people ranks 29th out of 50 states. In fact, with an average of 738 people per square mile (285 per sq km), Connecticut is one of the most crowded states in the country. Although most Nutmeggers live in cities, the attraction of the suburbs long ago began a major shift in population. Today, more than one-quarter of all Nutmeggers live in Fairfield County in the southwestern corner of the state, close to New York City.

Where Connecticuters Live

The colors on this map indicate population density throughout the state. The darker the color, the more people live there.

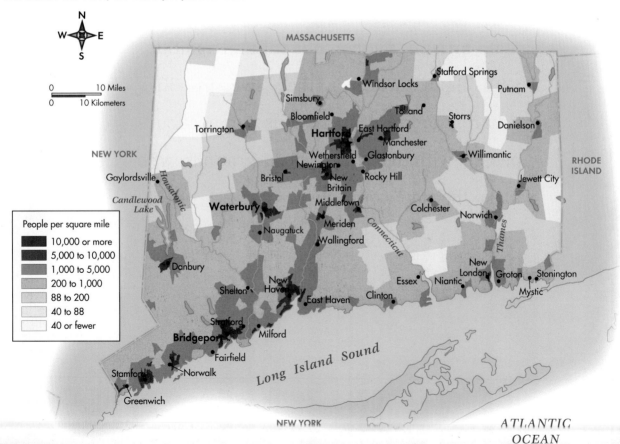

People QuickFacts

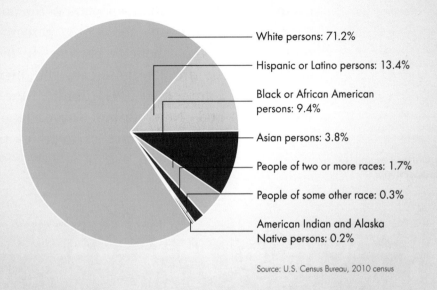

White persons: 71.2%

Hispanic or Latino persons: 13.4%

Black or African American persons: 9.4%

Asian persons: 3.8%

People of two or more races: 1.7%

People of some other race: 0.3%

American Indian and Alaska Native persons: 0.2%

Source: U.S. Census Bureau, 2010 census

A FLOOD OF IMMIGRANTS

Where do Connecticut's people come from? Some can trace their ancestors to the first Native people who settled in the area. Others have roots that go back to the early English colonists. Starting in the 1800s, waves of Irish, Germans, Swedes, Poles, Italians, and other Europeans arrived. Many of the first Italian immigrants found homes in Hartford and New Haven. Connecticut's Polish people settled in towns such as Meriden, Middletown, New Britain, and Norwich. African Americans from the South arrived in great numbers during World War II, going to

An Italian neighborhood in New Haven

work in Connecticut factories. Today, African Americans make up a little more than 9 percent of the population.

Latinos make up about 13 percent of the state's population. About 7 percent of the people in Connecticut are Puerto Rican, the highest percentage of any state. Hartford, New Haven, Waterbury, and New Britain have large Latino communities; and Stamford is home to thousands

Students at the Amistad Academy take part in a class activity.

Connecticut Population Growth

This chart shows Connecticut's population growth between 1790 and 2010.

Source: U.S. Census Bureau, 2010 census

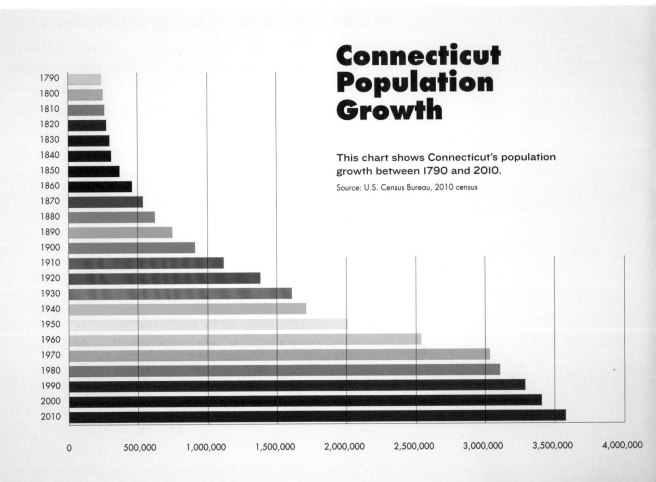

Year	Population

(Chart: Connecticut Population Growth, 1790–2010. Horizontal bars by decade from 1790 to 2010, scale 0 to 4,000,000.)

1790
1800
1810
1820
1830
1840
1850
1860
1870
1880
1890
1900
1910
1920
1930
1940
1950
1960
1970
1980
1990
2000
2010

0   500,000   1,000,000   1,500,000   2,000,000   2,500,000   3,000,000   3,500,000   4,000,000

of people from Guatemala. More recently, people from Mexico have come to the state.

Asians make up Connecticut's fastest-growing minority population, jumping nearly 65 percent between 2000 and 2010. Asians make up about 4 percent of the state's population. Many Asian newcomers are locating in the southeastern part of the state.

Tending greenhouse plants

HOW TO TALK LIKE A NUTMEGGER

People in Connecticut have their own unique phrases, pronunciations, and terms for things. For example, Connecticut settlers borrowed the name of England's famed River Thames and gave it to one of their own rivers in the eastern part of the state. But the English pronounce their river "Tems," while Nutmeggers insist the correct way to say it is "Thames," pronouncing the "th" as you would in thumb. Maybe you call it downtown, but enter any Connecticut city and you will have to ask for the "center" if you want to find the business district.

HOW TO EAT LIKE A NUTMEGGER

For an idea of the different kinds of food you can find in Connecticut, go to New Haven. Just a few of your restaurant choices are Turkish, Thai, Malaysian, Middle Eastern, and Ethiopian. Among New Haven's many claims to fame is the hamburger. Locals insist that this American classic was first served at Louis' (pronounced "Louie's") Lunch in 1900. There it's served on white toast with a slice of onion, tomato, or cheese. Visit New Britain's Polish neighborhood to sample delicious dishes such as *placki* (potato pancakes), pierogi (dumplings with fillings such as meat, potato, or cheese), or *golabki* (stuffed cabbage).

Connecticut's coastal location makes seafood popular, and many restaurants boast fresh catches of oysters, clams, lobsters, and a variety of fish.

People in Connecticut will be happy to debate where to find the best pizza in the world. Many visitors agree you can't beat the thin-crust, brick-oven pizza popular in New Haven.

Oyster

MENU

WHAT'S ON THE MENU IN CONNECTICUT?

Clam Chowder

Chowder got its name from the French word *chaudiere*, meaning "large kettle." You can't visit Connecticut and not have a bowl of New England clam chowder. It's a piping hot soup, thick with clams, potatoes, and onions, all chopped up.

Apples

Connecticut's abundant orchards produce many varieties of apples, which can be baked into pies, cakes, and muffins; added to salads; made into applesauce and cider; or eaten fresh from the tree.

Indian Pudding

You can thank the Native people for helping Connecticut colonists learn this recipe. This is a baked pudding made with milk, butter, molasses, cornmeal, and spices. Some people like to sprinkle raisins or sliced apples on top. Others serve it with a scoop of vanilla ice cream. Any way you eat this dessert, it's absolutely delicious.

TRY THIS RECIPE
Connecticut Chili Dog Sauce

A hot dog in a bun is not a Connecticut chili dog until it gets its special sauce. Here is the recipe. Be sure to have a grown-up nearby to help.

Ingredients:
1 small onion, chopped
1 garlic clove, crushed
1 tablespoon vegetable oil
1 pound ground beef
2 cups water
1 tablespoon chili powder
½ teaspoon cinnamon
1 teaspoon paprika
½ teaspoon nutmeg
½ teaspoon allspice
Salt and pepper to taste

Instructions:
Brown the onion and garlic in the oil. Add the ground beef and brown it, stirring to break up the meat. Add the water and the remaining ingredients. Let simmer 20 to 30 minutes, or until the mixture is thick and the water evaporates. Serve over a prepared hot dog on a bun, and you have a Connecticut chili dog.

Clam chowder

Apple cider

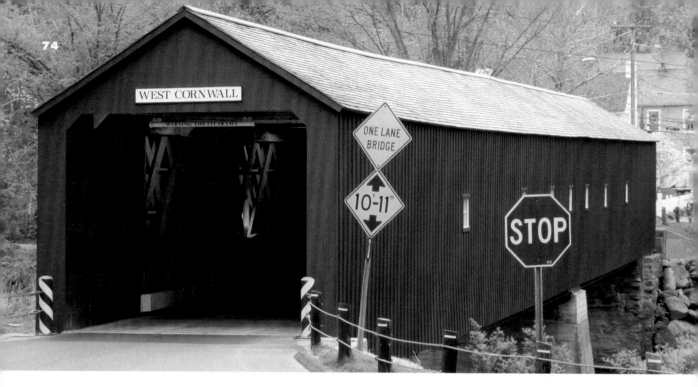

WEST CORNWALL

ONE LANE BRIDGE

10'-11"

STOP

West Cornwall Bridge is one of the most photographed places in Connecticut.

The oldest stone house in New England is the Henry Whitfield House in Guilford, built in 1639.

COVERED BRIDGES AND SALTBOX HOUSES

Many New England states are known for their historic covered bridges and colonial saltbox houses. More than 100 years ago, 18 covered bridges spanned Connecticut's Housatonic River. And Ithiel Town, an architect famous for his bridge design, was born in Connecticut. Why go to the trouble to cover a bridge? The roof and walls protect the wooden beams and planks from the sun and rain, keeping them from rotting as quickly as an open bridge. They are also pretty to look at and fun to cross. Three covered bridges still stand in Connecticut today. The oldest is Bull's Bridge in Kent, built in 1842. The bright red 1864 West Cornwall Bridge is the longest, at 242 feet (74 m). These two bridges incorporate Town's design. The 1872 Comstock Bridge over the Salmon River is not open for cars to cross, but you can still walk across it.

Have you ever seen a saltbox house? It is a building style that dates to the colonial period and is still popular throughout the United States. In colonial times, growing New England families often needed to add rooms on to their small two-story houses. So they built one-story additions at the back. The enlarged house with its long sloping roof looked like the boxes in which people kept their salt, giving the style its name. In Connecticut, some saltbox houses dating to the early 1700s are open to visitors.

SCHOOLS AND SPORTS

On South Street in Litchfield is the Tapping Reeve House and Law School. Today, it is a museum, but when Judge Tapping Reeve opened its doors in 1774, it was America's first law school. Dozens of future U.S. representatives studied here. So did U.S. vice presidents Aaron Burr and John C. Calhoun. Connecticuters have always valued education. Preparatory (prep) schools are private schools that prepare teenagers for college. Connecticut has plenty of those, including the Gunnery, in Washington, which is more than a century old. America's first all-girls prep school was Miss Porter's School in Farmington, founded in 1843.

An elementary school class dances to get energized and prepare for taking a long test.

In 2011, about 540,000 students in grades kindergarten through 12 were enrolled in Connecticut's public schools. About 30,000 were enrolled in the state's 368 private schools. The state has introduced programs to create more diversity in the public schools. One example is the Open Choice program, which allows students to attend public schools in nearby towns or cities.

Yale University in New Haven is one of the nation's best-known institutions of higher learning. Just a few of Yale's well-known graduates are inventor Samuel F. B. Morse, writer James Fenimore Cooper, actor Jodie Foster, and presidents William Howard Taft and both George H. W. Bush and George W. Bush. Former president Bill Clinton met his wife, Hillary, at Yale Law School. On the Yale campus, you will find colleges of art, architecture, drama, music, nursing, medicine, law, and business management. You will also find more than 15 million books and electronic volumes at the college libraries!

One of the nation's five military service academies is located in Connecticut. It is the U.S. Coast Guard Academy in New London. Since 1910, uniformed cadets

WOW

The American School for the Deaf in West Hartford was founded in 1817. It was the nation's first free school for children with hearing disabilities.

Students on the Yale University campus

there have been learning how to protect the U.S. waterways and coastline. The state's public colleges include the University of Connecticut (UConn), which has a renowned medical research center. Eastern, Western, Southern, and Central Connecticut State Universities are also major public schools. Altogether, there are more than 40 colleges, community colleges, and universities in the state. Approximately 80 percent of the state's high school graduates attend college.

UConn battles Boston University during a basketball tournament.

Sports fans never get bored in Connecticut! For great college basketball, head to Gampel Pavilion on the Storrs campus of UConn and watch the champion Huskies play. Both the men's and the women's teams have won the NCAA championship several times. Year after year, the school produces excellent teams. Up to 38,000 football fans pack Rentschler Field Stadium in East Hartford to watch UConn's Big East Conference team in action. The annual Yale-Harvard football game has been a tradition since 1875!

If snagging foul balls at a baseball game is more your style, Connecticut has several minor league teams throughout the state. They include the Norwich Navigators, the Bridgeport Bluefish, and the New Haven County Cutters. The Pilot Pen Tennis Tournament draws top professional players to Yale every August. And the roar of race-car engines attracts people to Stafford Motor Speedway in Stafford Springs and Lime Rock Park in Lakeville.

WALLACE STEVENS: THE INSURANCE MAN POET

For years, Wallace Stevens (1879–1955) walked back and forth to work in Hartford. It was 2 miles (3.2 km) from his home at 18 Westerly Terrace to his insurance office at the Hartford Accident and Indemnity Company on Ashley Avenue. While he walked, Stevens often played with words in his head. How many Hartford citizens could guess that the neatly dressed businessman was one of America's greatest poets? His first book of poems, *Harmonium,* appeared in 1923. His *Collected Poems* won the Pulitzer Prize in 1954.

Want to know more? Visit www.factsfornow.scholastic.com and enter the keyword **Connecticut**.

CONNECTICUT ARTS

Books have always been important to Connecticuters. Theophilus Eaton started the New Haven Public Library in 1886 with a gift of books. Puritan minister Jonathan Edwards was born in East Windsor, and many of his sermons were later published, including some from as early as 1741. In 1783, Jupiter Hammond of Hartford became America's first published African American poet. A group of writers called the Hartford Wits often met at the Bunch of Grapes Tavern to discuss literature after the Revolutionary War. Gathered around the table were writers such as John Trumbull (no relation to the state's first governor), Joel Barlow, and Lemuel Hopkins.

These days, Connecticut is home to several authors. They include Patricia Reilly Giff, a resident of Weston, whose *Lily's Crossing* and *Pictures of Hollis Woods* received Newbery Honors; and Suzy Kline, who calls West Willington home and whose Horrible Harry series is popular.

Charles Ives

Music, too, has been important to Connecticuters. Charles Ives was born in Danbury and is widely considered to be the first American classical composer of international significance. On the pop scene, John Mayer is a Grammy award-winning musician. Mark McGrath, lead singer for the rock band Sugar Ray, was born in Hartford, and Liz Phair, born in New Haven, is a singer-songwriter whose album *Exile in Guyville* was named one of *Rolling Stone* magazine's 500 greatest albums of all time.

Liz Phair performing in Boston

MINI-BIO

PAUL ROBESON: A VOICE FOR EQUALITY

Paul Robeson (1898–1976) was an athlete, scholar, lawyer, actor, and singer. After graduating from Rutgers and then Columbia Law School, he gained fame as a Broadway actor. His deep baritone voice attracted people to his many singing concerts. Robeson lived in Enfield, Connecticut, from 1940 to 1953. His singing career, however, took him all over the United States. Everywhere he went, he spoke out in favor of racial equality. "I stand here struggling for the rights of my people to be full citizens," he once exclaimed.

? Want to know more? Visit www.factsfornow.scholastic.com and enter the keyword **Connecticut**.

Connecticut resident Paul Newman (left) appears with Geraldine Page and Sidney Blackmer in a Broadway play.

MINI-BIO

EUGENE O'NEILL: PRIZEWINNING PLAYWRIGHT

Eugene O'Neill (1888–1953) spent his boyhood summers in New London, Connecticut. His father, James, had won fame as an actor playing the role of the Count of Monte Cristo and named their summer cottage Monte Cristo. As a playwright, Eugene won four Pulitzer Prizes for drama and the Nobel Prize for Literature in 1936. His play Ah, Wilderness! is a comedy that takes place in a summer cottage like Monte Cristo. His famous biographical tragedy Long Day's Journey into Night is set at Monte Cristo, too.

? **Want to know more?** Visit www.factsfornow .scholastic.com and enter the keyword **Connecticut**.

Connecticut is close to the Broadway theaters of New York City. For that reason, many playwrights and actors choose to live in the state. Until his death in 2005, playwright Arthur Miller lived in Roxbury. He wrote plays such as *Death of a Salesman* and *The Crucible*. Many classic plays had their first run in Connecticut. The musicals *Man of La Mancha, Annie,* and *Shenandoah* were all first performed at the Goodspeed Opera House in East Haddam before moving on to New York City. *My Fair Lady, A Streetcar Named Desire,* and *The Sound of Music* were all first performed at New Haven's Shubert Theater before wowing audiences on Broadway.

Artists in Connecticut have been busy since colonial times. Ralph Earl painted landscapes and portraits and had a studio in New Haven in 1775. Beginning in the 1820s, Thomas Cole painted beautiful scenes of Connecticut. So did Cole's talented student Frederic Church. Artist John Trumbull, son of Connecticut's first governor, painted thrilling scenes of the Revolutionary War. Some of his giant paintings now hang in the U.S. Capitol in Washington, D.C. Julian Alden Weir bought land in Wilton in 1882, and he invited other **impressionist** artists to stay at Weir Farm and paint. Elsie Driggs was a painter, born in Hartford in 1898, whose work is in the Whitney Museum of American Art in New York City. A contemporary conceptual artist, Mel Bochner is a professor at Yale, and his work is in the collection of the Museum of Modern Art in New York City.

WORD TO KNOW

impressionist *a style of art that gives a sense or impression of the object or scene being depicted*

Idle Hours, an 1888 work by painter Julian Alden Weir

READ ABOUT

Hannah Leahy
of Tolland
appears with
oceanographer
Robert Ballard at
the state capitol.

CHAPTER SEVEN

GOVERNMENT

★

BELIEVE IT OR NOT, YOU DO NOT HAVE TO BE AN ADULT TO BE A LAWYER IN CONNECTICUT. Just ask the young people who take part in mock trials every year. In a mock trial, students take on the roles of lawyers and witnesses for both sides of a case, researching the law and arguing the case. The Connecticut government sponsors this program to teach young people how the legal system works. There is a middle school competition and a high school competition, too.

From 1703 until 1875, Connecticut had two state capitals! One year, the General Assembly would meet in Hartford. The next year, it would meet in New Haven. Today, Hartford is the only capital.

THE STATE CAPITOL

You'll see the gold dome first, long before you get to 210 Capitol Avenue in Hartford. Workers completed Connecticut's capitol in 1878. Architect Richard Upjohn designed it, and in 1885 a group of architects declared the capitol "one of the ten best buildings in the United States." The offices of the executive branch of the state government are located there. So are the two chambers of the General Assembly. On display are memorabilia from the Revolutionary and Civil wars. The capitol grounds were designed by landscape architect Frederick Law Olmsted. Born in Hartford, Olmsted also designed the grounds of the U.S. Capitol in Washington, D.C., and Central Park in New York City.

The state capitol in Hartford

Capital City

This map shows places of interest in Hartford, Connecticut's capital city.

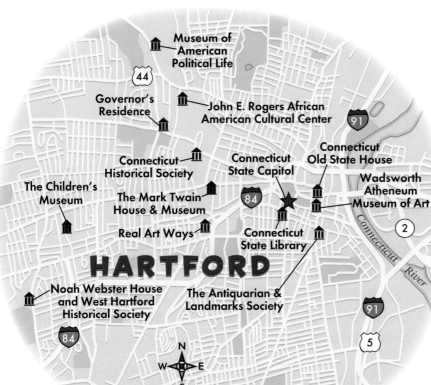

Museum of American Political Life

Governor's Residence

John E. Rogers African American Cultural Center

Connecticut Historical Society

Connecticut State Capitol

Connecticut Old State House

Wadsworth Atheneum Museum of Art

The Children's Museum

The Mark Twain House & Museum

Real Art Ways

Connecticut State Library

HARTFORD

Noah Webster House and West Hartford Historical Society

The Antiquarian & Landmarks Society

N W E S

Connecticut River

Capitol Facts

Here are some fascinating facts about Connecticut's state capitol.

Year it opened: 1879
Cost of construction: . . More than $2.5 million
Architect: . . . . Richard Upjohn
Style: . . . . High Victorian Gothic style
Latest renovation: 1979–1989
Dome: . . . . .Gold leaf
Exterior: . . . . .Marble from East Canaan, Connecticut, and granite from Westerly, Rhode Island

SEE IT HERE!

THE OLD STATE HOUSE

Be careful when you ask for directions to the capitol in Hartford. You might get sent to the Old State House at 800 Main Street by mistake. From 1796 until 1878, when the state capitol was completed, the Old State House was the center of Connecticut's government. It was the first specially built statehouse in the nation. Today, the building is a museum, full of curious things, such as a stuffed two-headed calf and a stuffed goat with three horns. Now those are sights worth telling your friends about!

HOW CONNECTICUT'S GOVERNMENT WORKS

In 1965, Connecticut voters ratified a new state constitution. The constitution describes how the state government must work. Like the U.S. government, Connecticut's government is divided into three branches: legislative, judicial, and executive. It is the job of the legislative branch to make the laws. The judicial branch **interprets** the laws, and the executive branch makes sure the laws are enforced.

THE LEGISLATIVE BRANCH

The lawmaking body is called the General Assembly. It consists of two houses. The upper house is the senate, and the lower house is the house of representatives. New assembly members are elected every two years. The

WORD TO KNOW

interprets *explains the meaning of*

Members of the Connecticut House of Representatives take the oath of office.

Governor Dannel Malloy speaks in front of the General Assembly in Hartford in 2013.

senate must have at least 30 but no more than 50 members. Its members include a president pro tempore (the leader of the majority political party) and a clerk. The house of representatives must contain at least 125 but no more than 225 members. These legislators choose their own speaker, a clerk, and other officers. The regular session of the General Assembly begins on the Wednesday following the first Monday of January.

Each house of the assembly determines its own rules and keeps a journal of its daily activities. General Assembly members form committees to consider new bills. Bills are submitted by committee or by individual assembly members for general consideration. When they have been passed by a majority of both houses, the bills are sent to the governor's office for approval.

DANNEL MALLOY: OVERCOMING OBSTACLES

As a child, Dannel Malloy (1955–) had learning disabilities that made schoolwork a tough challenge. Doctors diagnosed his condition, and he learned how to succeed in school. Malloy developed a great memory, which he used to graduate with honors from Boston College Law School. He served as a lawyer in New York City from 1980 to 1984, and then ran successfully for mayor of Stamford. In 2010, he ran for the office of governor and won. With the state facing tough financial times, Malloy was forced to raise taxes, including those on income and gasoline.

? Want to know more? Visit www.factsfornow .scholastic.com and enter the keyword **Connecticut**.

THE JUDICIAL BRANCH

The judicial branch is the state's court system. The Connecticut Supreme Court is the state's highest court. The governor nominates seven justices for this court—a chief justice and six associate justices—and the General Assembly must approve them. They serve eight-year terms. A justice can be removed from office if the assembly votes by a two-thirds majority to do so. The state supreme court meets as many as eight times each year for about two or three weeks at a time.

Lower courts also hear legal cases. These courts include superior court judges (who serve eight-year terms), probate court judges (four-year terms), and justices of the peace (four-year terms). Judges are elected to all of these offices by the General Assembly. No justice of the peace may hold office after the age of 70. Many of the higher court judges must also retire at that age.

THE EXECUTIVE BRANCH

The governor is the head of the executive branch. Every four years in November, voters elect a governor. The governor must be at least 30 years old, and he or she can serve two terms in a row. Other members of the executive branch who are elected include the lieutenant governor, secretary of state, treasurer, and comptroller. The lieutenant governor presides over the senate. The gover-

Connecticut's State Government

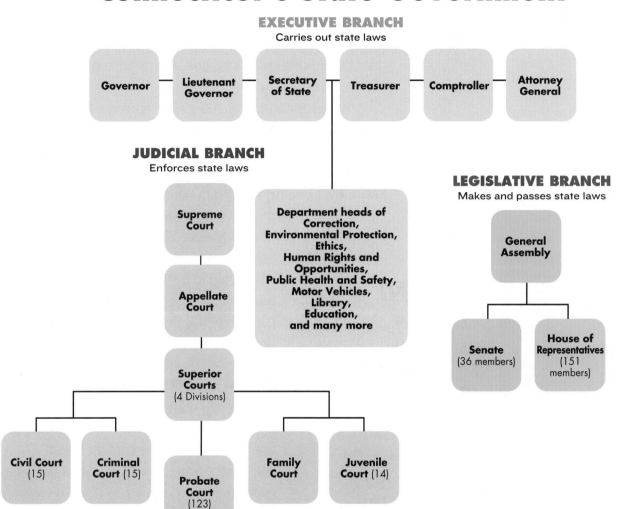

EXECUTIVE BRANCH
Carries out state laws

Governor | Lieutenant Governor | Secretary of State | Treasurer | Comptroller | Attorney General

JUDICIAL BRANCH
Enforces state laws

Supreme Court

Appellate Court

Superior Courts (4 Divisions)

Department heads of Correction, Environmental Protection, Ethics, Human Rights and Opportunities, Public Health and Safety, Motor Vehicles, Library, Education, and many more

Civil Court (15) | Criminal Court (15) | Probate Court (123) | Family Court | Juvenile Court (14)

LEGISLATIVE BRANCH
Makes and passes state laws

General Assembly

Senate (36 members) | House of Representatives (151 members)

Representing Connecticut

This list shows the number of elected officials who represent Connecticut, both on the state and national levels.

OFFICE	NUMBER	LENGTH OF TERM
State senators	36	2 years
State house members	151	2 years
U.S. senators	2	6 years
U.S. representatives	5	2 years
Presidential electors	7	—

nor selects additional officers for the executive branch, and these choices must be approved by the assembly.

The main duty of the executive branch is to carry out the state's laws. The governor oversees many state agencies and offices.

When the General Assembly writes a new law, the bill is submitted to the governor. The governor may veto, or turn down, any new law made by the legislature. The legislature then has a chance to overturn the governor's veto, by a two-thirds vote in both houses. In Connecticut, the governor also has the power of the line-item veto. This means that the governor may turn down specific parts of any bill having to do with the spending of state money. After cutting out disapproved parts of a bill, the governor may still sign the rest of the bill into law.

LOCAL GOVERNMENT

There are 8 counties, 21 cities, 169 towns, and 9 boroughs in Connecticut. A borough is a town whose government is run like a business. Connecticut's counties have no governments. The state's cities and towns have their own governments, typically led by mayors or selectmen. It is the duty of local officials to carry out the wishes of the voters. Many towns in the state still hold town meetings, like the English colonists used to long ago. Adult taxpayers can attend. They may address town officials. You could say local government in Connecticut is the most basic form of democracy in action!

MINI-BIO

ELLA GRASSO: THE FIRST WOMAN GOVERNOR

Ella Grasso (1919–1981) was born in Windsor Locks. A Democrat, she was elected to the state legislature in 1952 and later served three terms as Connecticut's secretary of state. She served two terms in the U.S. Congress from 1970 to 1974. Then in 1974, she became the first woman in the United States to be elected governor, having not succeeded her husband in office. During her six years as governor, she kept her promise never to establish state income taxes.

? **Want to know more?** Visit www.factsfornow .scholastic.com and enter the keyword **Connecticut**.

CONNECTICUT'S PRESIDENTS

George H. W. Bush (1924–) was born in Massachusetts but grew up in Greenwich. After serving as vice president under Ronald Reagan (1981–1989), he was elected the 41st U.S. president (1989–1993). He organized Operation Desert Storm to free Kuwait from Iraqi invasion during the Persian Gulf War.

George W. Bush (1946–) was born in New Haven, the son of George H. W. Bush. After serving as governor of Texas (1995–2000), he was elected the 43rd U.S. president in 2000 and reelected to a second term in 2004.

Connecticut Counties

This map shows the 8 counties in Connecticut. Hartford, the state capital, is indicated with a star.

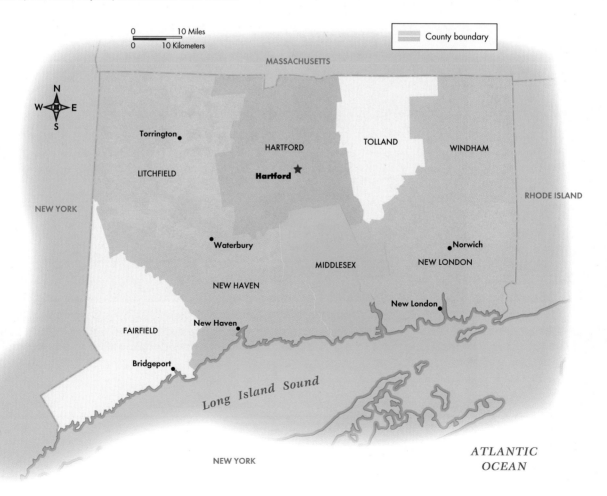

State Flag

The Connecticut flag was adopted in 1897. It has a background of blue, against which is the state seal in white and natural colors; the border of the seal is embroidered in gold and silver. Below the seal is a white streamer bearing in dark blue the motto *Qui Transtulit Sustinet*, which means "He who transplanted still sustains."

State Seal

Connecticut's first seal was brought from England by Colonel George Fenwick in 1639. Over the years, the seal was altered a number of times. Today's version features three grapevines, which may represent the original colonies of Saybrook, New Haven, and Hartford that went on to become the state of Connecticut. The phrase *Sigillum Reipublicae Connecticutensis* means "Seal of the State of Connecticut."

READ ABOUT

Fritz Knipschildt
shows off some
of the chocolates
and other treats
that are handmade
at his Knipschildt
Chocolatier
in Norwalk.

CHAPTER EIGHT

ECONOMY

★

PERHAPS YOU HAVE WASHED CARS OR CUT A NEIGHBOR'S LAWN FOR MONEY? Or sold lemonade at a sidewalk stand? People who sell a product or provide a service are participating in their economy. Connecticut's businesses and factories are the strength of the state's economy. Insurance companies, farms, and other industries add to it, too. In the end, success depends on hard work. When their alarm clocks ring each day, Connecticuters get up and head off to all kinds of interesting jobs.

350 YEARS OF FARMING HISTORY

Breathe deeply and smell the salty air. The Davis Farm lies at the mouth of the Pawcatuck River in southeastern Connecticut. Each summer and fall, you can see tall, yellow salt grass growing on the 400 acres (162 ha). When cold weather arrives, the crop is cut and raked by hand into piles of salt hay. The same family has been farming the land for 350 years! The farmhouse was built in the 1670s, and the Davis family hopes to preserve it as a museum one day.

High school students tend tomato plants at the Connecticut Agricultural Experiment Station in Hamden.

AGRICULTURE

Visit the campus of the University of Connecticut at Storrs, and you might see cows grazing on the grass nearby. They are part of the school's agricultural program. Farming has always been important in Connecticut. In 2011, there were 2,273 farmers in Connecticut. They carry on a proud farming tradition that began in the 1600s. Across the state's rolling landscape are 400,000 acres (160,000 ha) of farmland. That represents 13 percent of all the land in the state. Today, there are 4,900 farms in Connecticut, with an average size of 82 acres (33 ha). Nursery items such as trees and flowers top the list of what's grown on these farms. Milk, cheese, and other dairy products are important, too. Connecticut produces more eggs, pears, peaches, and mushrooms than any other New England state!

Major Agricultural and Mining Products

This map shows where Connecticut's major agricultural and mining products come from. See a chicken? That means poultry is found there.

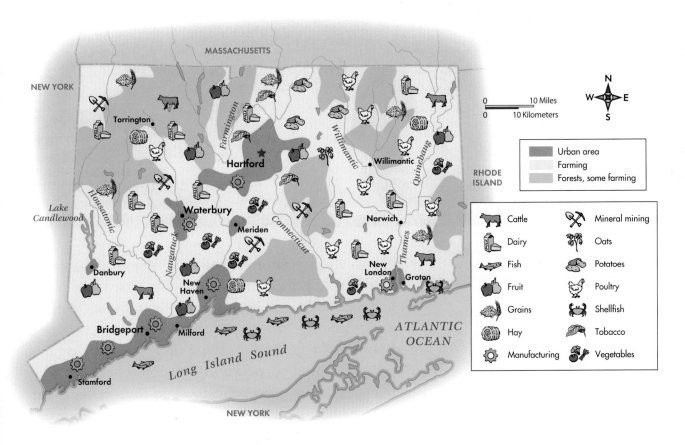

Legend:
- Urban area
- Farming
- Forests, some farming

Cattle		Mineral mining	
Dairy		Oats	
Fish		Potatoes	
Fruit		Poultry	
Grains		Shellfish	
Hay		Tobacco	
Manufacturing		Vegetables	

MANUFACTURING INDUSTRY

Throughout its history, Connecticut has been a manufacturing state. In 1790, the U.S. **Patent** Office opened in Washington, D.C. New inventions are registered there. Since it opened, it has granted patents to more inventors and companies from Connecticut than from any other state.

WORD TO KNOW

patent *an official document giving only to an inventor the right to make, use, or sell the invention for a certain number of years*

A worker operates an inserting machine that prints addresses and stacks materials at a mail-sorting facility in Windsor.

WOW

Pratt, Read, & Company, founded in Essex, was for many years the busiest maker of piano keys in the United States!

Elias Howe invented the first practical sewing machine in Connecticut in 1845. The first truly portable typewriter was invented by Stamford's George C. Blickensderfer in 1889. Connecticuters Albert Pope and Hiram Maxim began selling their electric cars in 1897. In fact, by 1900, nearly 10,000 different manufacturing companies were in business in Connecticut. In Connecticut in the 20th century, Edwin P. Land developed the Polaroid camera, which makes instant photographs, in the state. Peter Goldmark developed color television in Connecticut, too.

Today, Connecticut factory workers produce sewing machines, motors, hardware and tools, knives, clocks, and locks. Electronics and computer equipment are both growing and important industries. Highly skilled workers make Connecticut a leader among states as a maker of finished metals and plastics. Connecticut is the world headquarters of such corporate giants as Xerox, General Electric, and Uniroyal. With about 202,000 workers in manufacturing, Connecticut will continue to provide Americans with valued manufactured products for many years to come.

THE DEFENSE INDUSTRY

Connecticut has long been known for its defense industry. Igor Sikorsky started an aircraft company there in 1923. Today, Sikorsky Aircraft Corporation's 18,000 workers produce military helicopters such as the UH-60 Black Hawk. Since 1957, the U.S. president's official helicopter,

A Sikorsky UH-60M Black Hawk helicopter at the Sikorsky Aircraft plant in Stratford in 2006

MINI-BIO

IGOR SIKORSKY: MAKING A DREAM COME TRUE

"Even in my childhood . . . I dreamed about the possibility of going straight up," said Igor Sikorsky (1889–1972). Before he came to the United States from the Ukraine in 1919, he was a successful airplane designer. He settled in Bridgeport and developed an aircraft with a spinning blade on top. On September 14, 1939, the Vought-Sikorsky 300 successfully flew for the first time. It rose straight up into the air. Sikorsky had invented the helicopter. Today, the Sikorsky Aircraft Corporation in Stratford is one of the world's leading makers of helicopters.

? Want to know more? Visit www.factsfornow .scholastic.com and enter the keyword **Connecticut.**

Marine One, has been made by Sikorsky. Francis Pratt and Amos Whitney started a machine shop in Hartford in 1860; today, more than 35,000 people work for Pratt & Whitney Aircraft at locations around the world, making engines for the U.S. Air Force's F-22 Raptor fighter jet, among other products.

The USS *Nautilus* was developed in Groton. Launched in 1954, it became the world's first nuclear-powered submarine. The Electric Boat Company, with main operations in Groton, employs more than 10,000 workers who design and make submarines for the U.S. Navy. Other Connecticut companies that supply America's military include Northrop Grumman Norden Systems (radar for spy planes), Transatlantic Lines (cargo and transport services), and the Barnes Group (engine parts).

MINING AND FISHING

Copper, iron, nickel, and garnet were all minerals once dug out of Connecticut's mines. Brownstone quarried in Portland was used in buildings as far away as New Orleans, Louisiana. Today, only about 60 mines remain in operation in Connecticut. Almost all of them are surface mines, not deep tunnels in the ground. Connecticut's miners quarry stone, gravel, sand, and clay. Sand can be heated and formed into glass. Heated and glazed, clay becomes ceramic dishes, plates, and cups.

With so much coastline along Long Island Sound, Connecticut has a huge commercial fishing industry. The state is one of the country's top producers of oysters, which are found in tidal rivers, coastal bays, and farms in Long Island Sound. Lobster

Top Products

Agriculture Greenhouse and nursery products, dairy products

Manufacturing Transportation equipment, fabricated metals

Mining Sand and gravel, traprock

Fishing Scallops, skates, lobsters

A fishing boat dredges for oysters in Long Island Sound.

is caught in lobster pots along the sound. Flounder, shad, and other fish are netted by coastal fishing boats. In 2010, Connecticut's fishers caught 6,015,000 pounds (2,728,000 kilograms) of fish in the sound to eat. That's $17.1 million worth of fish!

SERVICE INDUSTRIES

Hotels, hospitals, and insurance companies are all examples of service industries, or businesses that provide services. Hotels offer temporary lodging, and hospitals provide medical care. Insurance companies sell protection to minimize financial loss because of accidents.

In 1794, a few Hartford residents were offering insurance to other residents to protect their homes against fire. In 1810, the Hartford Fire Insurance Company started writing regular policies. The nationwide insurance industry had begun. As the years passed, Connecticut insurance companies began offering other kinds of policies to protect people and property. These included life, accident, and health insurance. For just two cents, the Travelers Insurance Company issued the first auto **insurance policy** in 1898.

In the 1960s, Connecticut was known as the insurance capital of the world. In recent years, some Hartford insurance companies have merged with companies

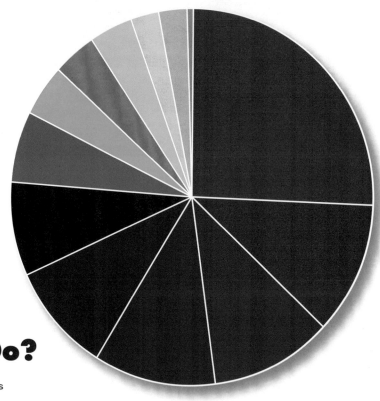

What Do Connecticuters Do?

This color-coded chart shows what industries Connecticuters work in.

25.6% Educational services, and health care and social assistance, 451,766

11.4% Manufacturing, 201,999

11.0% Retail trade, 193,940

10.8% Professional, scientific, and management, and administrative and waste management services, 190,314

9.5% Finance and insurance, and real estate and rental and leasing, 166,839

8.1% Arts, entertainment, and recreation, and accommodation and food services, 142,250

6.1% Construction, 107,614

4.5% Other services, except public administration, 79,787

3.8% Transportation and warehousing, and utilities, 67,041

3.8% Public administration, 66,776

2.6% Wholesale trade, 45,358

2.5% Information, 44,581

0.4% Agriculture, forestry, fishing and hunting, and mining, 6,490

Source: U.S. Census Bureau, 2010 census

from out of state. But the insurance industry is still one of the city's largest employers, providing more than 50,000 jobs. The Aetna Insurance Company, the Hartford, and the Phoenix Companies are three of the largest employers.

Connecticut's real estate industry has become a bigger business than insurance. Each year, billions of dollars change hands in the buying and selling of homes, buildings, and land.

Tourism is also big business in the state, bringing in about $11.5 billion a year. Among the state's popular tourist spots are the Foxwoods Resort Casino, owned by the Pequots, and the Mohegan Sun casino, owned by Mohegans. Other area attractions, such as museums, nature trails, and theaters, draw tourists and dollars into the state. Do you want to learn about some other interesting places that attract visitors to Connecticut? Turn the page and start reading Chapter 9!

PEQUOT ACTIVIST

In the 1960s, the Connecticut government tried to seize the last 213 acres (85 ha) of Pequot reservation land to make a state park. Elizabeth George (1894–1973), one of the only Pequots still living on the land, refused to surrender the property that belonged to her people. When bulldozers arrived, she stood in the road. "You're not going to plow up this ground," she insisted. "This is mine." George urged her family to carry on her fight. "Hold on to the land," she told them. The Pequots finally won their legal battle, and several years later they built Foxwoods Resort Casino, the largest and most successful casino in the world. Its profits go to the Pequot people.

A hiker in Hamden

CHAPTER NINE
TRAVEL GUIDE

TRAVEL GUIDE

★

FROM CORNER TO CORNER, THE STATE OF CONNECTICUT IS FILLED WITH WONDERS. Take a trip to Bridgeport and learn about showman P. T. Barnum. Stop at Mystic and imagine the life of an 1850s sailor at bustling Mystic Seaport. Climb into a fighter plane at the New England Air Museum, or have a relaxing picnic beside the waterfall in Kent Falls State Park. Grab your map and tour some of Connecticut's best places!

← Follow along with this travel map. We'll begin in Thomaston and travel around until we get to Stamford!

LITCHFIELD HILLS

THINGS TO DO: Ride a railroad car, explore a re-created 1600s Algonquian village, or take a swim.

Thomaston

★ **Railroad Museum of New England:** Climb aboard a railroad car and take a 20-mile (32 km) ride. Roar past the beautiful upland hills of western Connecticut. The leaves blaze fiery colors in the fall. Thomaston was named for the famous clockmaker Seth Thomas.

Kent

★ **Kent Falls State Park:** Feel the spray of the splashing water at the state's most spectacular waterfalls. The three cascades of Kent Falls drop 250 feet (76 m) over the course of a quarter mile (.4 km). After a picnic lunch, wade in the water and look for minnows.

Kent Falls State Park

Lake Compounce Theme Park

Bristol

★ **Lake Compounce Theme Park:** The whole family will enjoy the rides, including Boulder Dash, a wooden roller coaster. And don't miss Splash Harbor, the state's biggest water park.

★ **The New England Carousel Museum:** Hang on tight to your wooden horse as you ride the Bushnell Park Carousel. The wooden animals you'll see on exhibit are all works of highly skilled wood-carvers.

★ **American Clock & Watch Museum:** Discover the history of watches with this unique collection, from the earliest grandfather clocks to the Mickey Mouse wristwatch.

Goshen

★ **The Action Wildlife Foundation:**
Feed some of the 170 different
kinds of animals that live in this
game park. They include zebras,
yaks, and llamas. And would you
believe fainting goats? Under
stress, the goats freeze up and fall
over on their sides!

Washington

★ **Institute for American Indian
Studies:** Ten thousand years of
Native American history, all in one
place. Walk the paths of a re-
created 1600s Algonquian village,
crouch inside a longhouse, or hike
the nature trails. In the garden,
you can see exactly how the
Algonquin grew their crops.

Institute for American Indian Studies

Middlebury

★ **Quassy Amusement Park:** This
20-acre (8 ha) family park on Lake
Quassapaug offers rides and games,
swimming, and live entertainment.

Waterbury

★ **Mattatuck Museum:** Learn more
about the history of Connecticut
industry at this museum, which
features 19th- and 20th-century art.

Litchfield

★ **White Memorial Conservation
Center:** At 4,000 acres (1,600
ha), it's the state's largest wildlife
refuge. Bring your bathing suit,
hiking boots, and binoculars,
because swimming, hiking, and
bird watching are a must here.

★ **Litchfield History Museum:** Take
a journey to the past to explore the
clothing, furniture, and artwork of
the city of Litchfield. Seven galleries showcase 18th-century family
life and work when the town was a
commercial and political center of
the region.

Ridgefield

★ **The Aldrich Contemporary Art Museum:** This museum is home to 12 galleries, a screening room, an education center, and a sculpture garden.

Brookfield

★ **Candlewood Lake:** This human-made lake was formed in the 1920s, when the Rocky River was dammed to create hydroelectric power. As a result, entire towns and farms disappeared beneath the water. Scuba divers claim they can sometimes see old roads and abandoned farmhouses on the lake's bottom.

Danbury

★ **Danbury Railway Museum:** Exhibits at this museum are displayed inside a former railway station, which was built in 1903. Outside there is a railroad yard full of railroad cars and equipment.

Candlewood Lake

RIVER VALLEY

THINGS TO DO: Take the controls of a historic airplane, climb aboard a trolley and ride the rails, or visit homes of noted authors.

Barkhamsted

★ **Kasulaitis Farm and Sugarhouse:** Maple cookies, maple candy, and, of course, maple syrup—you can get it all here. Visit during February or March and see the entire syrup-making process, from tree to bottle.

Connecticut's sugar maple trees produce 12,000 gallons (45,400 l) of maple syrup each year!

Hartford

★ **The Museum of Connecticut History:** Check out the extensive collection of about 1,000 Colt firearms, just one of the many exhibits here. Cowboys and sheriffs throughout the American West carried the famous Colt .45.

★ **The Harriet Beecher Stowe Center:** Tour this historic home and gardens to learn more about the author of *Uncle Tom's Cabin.*

★ **The Mark Twain House &
Museum:** This national historic
landmark is located in a Victorian
home where the author lived for
17 years. The 19 furnished rooms
feature pieces by Louis Comfort
Tiffany and many of Twain's
possessions.

Windsor Locks

★ **New England Air Museum:**
Climb into the cockpit of a jet
fighter plane. This museum boasts
75 different kinds of aircraft. The
oldest is a Bleriot IX airplane
dating from 1909.

The New England Air Museum

East Windsor

★ **Connecticut Trolley Museum:**
See a collection of 30 trolley cars
dating from 1892 to 1947. Imagine
the days before modern mass
transportation. Then take a seat
on a working trolley and enjoy a
3-mile (5-km) ride.

Stafford Motor Speedway

Stafford Springs

★ **Stafford Motor Speedway:** Watch
NASCAR race cars roar along the
.5-mile (.8 km) oval track. Hear the
tires squeal, and marvel at the pit
crews in action.

Rocky Hill

★ **Dinosaur State Park:** See dinosaur tracks from the Jurassic
period and hike the nature trails of
this national historic landmark.

East Haddam

★ **Gillette Castle:** Actor William Gillette lived in this stone castle overlooking the Connecticut River. The 184-acre (74 ha) estate has hiking trails and picnic spots.

Gillette Castle on the Connecticut River

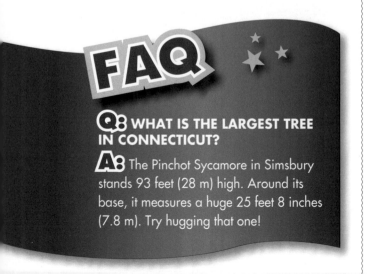

FAQ

Q: **WHAT IS THE LARGEST TREE IN CONNECTICUT?**

A: The Pinchot Sycamore in Simsbury stands 93 feet (28 m) high. Around its base, it measures a huge 25 feet 8 inches (7.8 m). Try hugging that one!

Simsbury

★ **Massacoh Plantation:** Life sure was different 250 years ago. A 1740 schoolhouse, a colonial barn, a carriage shed, and a cottage are just a few of the buildings you can explore here. Buy a piece of old-fashioned rock candy or a penny-whistle at the gift shop.

Wethersfield

★ **The Webb-Deane-Stevens Museum, the Hurlbut-Dunham House, the Captain James Francis House, and the Buttolph-Williams House:** These historic homes help give the town an authentic colonial look. All of them are furnished to look as they did more than 200 years ago.

Essex

★ **The Griswold Inn:** A stroll along Main Street reveals what a river town looked like more than a century ago. Afterward, stop at the historic Griswold Inn for some clam chowder. Listen to a guitarist sing old whaling songs. The Griswold Inn has been serving meals since 1776.

Glastonbury

★ **Glastonbury-Rocky Hill Ferry:**
Hurry aboard, the ferry's about to
leave! Enjoy the nation's oldest
continuously operated ferry on a
ride across the Connecticut River.
Boats have been carrying passengers across the river since 1665.

MYSTIC COUNTRY

**THINGS TO DO: Learn about
a Revolutionary War hero,
visit some marine animals, or tour an old
lighthouse.**

Storrs

★ **The Connecticut Archaeology
Center and Museum of Natural
History:** See what Connecticuters
have dug out of the ground over
the years at this museum located
on the University of Connecticut
campus. Visit during Archaeology
Month in October, and clean
ancient pieces of pottery or make a
fire using prehistoric-style tools.

Tolland

★ **Old Tolland County Jail and
Museum:** Walk inside a cell and
sit on a hard bunk. When the door
clanks shut, you'll know what it's like
to be locked up. The guides have lots
of stories to tell about this jail, which
was in use from 1856 until 1960.

Coventry

★ **Nathan Hale State Forest:** The
Nathan Hale Homestead is located
here. In July, join Revolutionary
War reenactors when they set up
camp here.

Creamery Brook Bison

Brooklyn

★ **Creamery Brook Bison:** Climb
aboard a tractor-pulled wagon and
tour this working farm. In one
pasture, a herd of 100 shaggy bison
(American buffalo) graze. Cows and
calves come so close you can feed
them hay.

Willimantic

★ **Windham Textile & History Museum:** In the 1870s, busy textile machinery thumped and whined here. Learn the complete story by walking inside the factory buildings and the re-created manager's mansion, workers' housing, and company store. Willimantic used to be called Thread City because of its many textile mills.

Canterbury

★ **Prudence Crandall Museum:** Walk inside the mansion that served as Prudence Crandall's school for girls in the 1830s. When she admitted African American girls, the townspeople forced her to close the school. Fascinating exhibits tell Crandall's story.

Stonington

★ **Old Lighthouse Museum:** This is one of 13 lighthouses in the state. Built in 1823, its light guided ships safely along the rocky coast. The view of Long Island Sound from the top is breathtaking.

Old Lighthouse Museum

Mystic

★ **Mystic Aquarium:** Plan to get wet on a visit here. More than 3,500 fish and other sea creatures make the aquarium their home. A great white shark circles inside a tank. Dolphins leap through hoops at the Marine Theater. Feed a seal or a penguin, or steer the remote controls of a device that will let you explore a shipwreck.

Mystic Seaport

★ **Mystic Seaport:** Climb aboard an old boat for a Mystic River cruise. The coal-fed *Sabino* chugs through the green water all summer long, with a guide describing the delightful river views. The *Resolute* is a smaller wooden motor launch, so get ready to rock with every wave.

★ **Denison Pequotsepos Nature Center:** Walk the self-guided tour of this 200-acre (80 ha) nature preserve. Find a hooting horned owl high in a tree. Discover frogs croaking in their bog. Toads, turtles, birds, and perhaps even a muskrat are waiting for you to take their pictures.

Groton

★ **Submarine Force Library & Museum:** Ahoy! Step aboard the USS *Nautilus*, the world's first nuclear-powered submarine. Climb belowdecks and see how submariners live. In the museum, operate a submarine yourself on an interactive computer display.

GREATER NEW HAVEN

THINGS TO DO: Hit the beach, learn about dinosaurs, or enjoy watching coastal birds in their native habitat.

Milford

★ **Connecticut Audubon Coastal Center:** This 8.4-acre (3.3 ha) wildlife sanctuary is located on Long Island Sound and is home to herons, ospreys, egrets, piping plovers, and many other feathered creatures.

Madison

★ **Hammonasset Beach State Park:** A million people can't be wrong. That's how many people each year enjoy the 3 miles (4.8 km) of beach-front located here. Splash in the salty waves, pitch a tent and camp, hike among the sand dunes, or go fishing, boating, or even scuba diving. This park has it all!

Hammonasset Beach State Park

New Haven

★ **Yale Peabody Museum of Natural History:** The dinosaur collection boasts a skeleton of a 67-foot (20 m) *Apatosaurus*, among other wonders. Visitors can touch a 100-million-year-old fossil, stand back-to-back with a full-size stuffed black bear, and spot all 16 of the museum's live poison dart frogs in their rain forest habitat.

★ **Yale University:** Tour this historic campus, dating from 1701, where Nathan Hale, Noah Webster, and many other notables once studied.

COASTAL FAIRFIELD

THINGS TO DO: Learn about a circus legend, visit an island, or take a nature hike.

Bridgeport

★ **Beardsley Zoo:** The state's only zoo is home to animals from North and South America, including some endangered species. It includes a tropical rain forest, a New England farmyard, and a carousel.

SEE IT HERE!

THE BARNUM MUSEUM

P. T. Barnum lived in Bridgeport for many years. In fact, at one time he was the town's mayor. But he was most famous as a circus owner. At The Barnum Museum at 820 Main Street, see how the great showman entertained Americans for years. Decide for yourself if Barnum's "Feejee Mermaid" was real. Learn about Jenny Lind, whose singing won her the nickname the Swedish Nightingale. Gaze at a model circus containing more than 3,000 little hand-carved figures. "Hurry, hurry, hurry," Barnum seems to call, "and see the many marvels!"

★ **Discovery Museum and Planetarium:** Visitors experiment with physical science here. Pull a crank, push a button, turn a lever, and see how your energy is put to work. Pedal a bicycle and create enough electricity to run a radio. Also connected with the museum is the Henry B. duPont Planetarium. Gaze at the night sky, or put on a space suit and join a crew on a Mars space expedition.

Greenwich

★ **Bruce Museum:** This museum offers marine touch tanks, changing environmental exhibits, and an education center.

Westport

★ **Earthplace, the Nature Discovery Center:** After walking the outdoor nature trails, learn about the care of animals by doing puzzles and handling scientific equipment. Help nurse an injured bird, dog, cat, or perhaps even a wild animal in the rehabilitation center.

A climbing exhibit at Discovery Museum

Norwalk

★ **SONO Switch Tower Museum:** Climb to the top of the switch tower high above the railroad tracks. Pull the switch levers, and the tracks move and the signal lights blink on the main line. Clap your hands over your ears as trains roar by beneath you, blowing their whistles.

Shark tank at The Maritime Aquarium

★ **The Maritime Aquarium:** Watch river otters, harbor seals, and sea turtles in action. Or take in a movie at the IMAX theater.

★ **Sheffield Island:** Take a boat trip to this island and see the lighthouse that dates to 1868.

Stamford

★ **Stamford Museum & Nature Center:** On 118 acres (48 ha), you'll find hiking trails, a picnic area, a New England working farm, and a boardwalk. The museum features interactive displays and a planetarium.

★ **Bartlett Arboretum & Gardens:** This 91-acre (37 ha) nature preserve includes lawns and formal gardens, 10 woodland hiking trails, a red maple wetland, a 3-acre (1.2 ha) wildflower meadow, and a greenhouse. There are education programs and a horticulture resource library.

WRITING PROJECTS

Check out these ideas for creating campaign brochures, writing you-are-there editorials, and researching early explorers to the state.

118

ART PROJECTS

Create a great PowerPoint presentation, illustrate the state song, or learn about the state quarter and design your own.

119

TIMELINE

What happened when? This timeline highlights important events in the state's history—and shows what was happening throughout the United States at the same time.

122

FAST FACTS

Use this section to find fascinating facts about state symbols, land area and population statistics, weather, sports teams, and much more.

126

GLOSSARY

Remember the Words to Know from the chapters in this book? They're all collected here.

125

SCIENCE, TECHNOLOGY, ENGINEERING, & MATH PROJECTS

120

Make weather maps, graph population statistics, and research endangered species that live in the state.

PRIMARY VS. SECONDARY SOURCES

121

So what are primary and secondary sources? And what's the diff? This section explains all that and where you can find them.

BIOGRAPHICAL DICTIONARY

133

This at-a-glance guide highlights some of the state's most important and influential people. Visit this section and read about their contributions to the state, the country, and the world.

RESOURCES

Books and much more. Take a look at these additional sources for information about the state.

138

WRITING PROJECTS

Write a Memoir, Journal, or Editorial for Your School Newspaper!

Picture Yourself . . .

★ Traveling through the wilderness. You've set out from Massachusetts in 1636 with 100 others to make the 100-mile (160 km) journey to Hartford, with only a compass to guide you. Everything you own is in the pack on your back. Keep a journal of your trip.

SEE: Chapter Two, pages 20–29.

★ Living in a colonial settlement in the early 1700s. What would your days be like? And how would you get essential goods?

SEE: Chapter Three, pages 35–37.

Create an Election Brochure or Web Site!

Run for office! Throughout this book you've read about some of the issues that concern Connecticut today.

★ As a candidate for governor of Connecticut, create a campaign brochure or Web site.

★ Explain how you meet the qualifications to be governor of Connecticut, and talk about the three or four major issues you'll focus on if you are elected.

★ Remember, you'll be responsible for Connecticut's budget! How would you spend the taxpayers' money?

SEE: Chapter Seven, pages 82–90.

Compare and Contrast —When, Why, and How Did They Come?

Compare the migration and explorations of the first Native people and the first European explorers. Tell about:

    ★ When their migrations began
    ★ How they traveled
    ★ Why they migrated
    ★ Where their journeys began and ended
    ★ What they found when they arrived

SEE: Chapters Two and Three, pages 20–37.

Thomas Hooker leading a group into Connecticut

ART PROJECTS

Create a PowerPoint Presentation or Visitors' Guide

Welcome to Connecticut!

Connecticut's a great place to visit and to live! From its natural beauty to its bustling cities and historic sites, there's plenty to see and do. In your PowerPoint presentation or brochure, highlight 10 to 15 of Connecticut's stunnning landmarks. Be sure to include:

★ a map of the state showing where these sites are located

★ photos, illustrations, Web links, natural history facts, geographic stats, climate and weather info, and descriptions of plants and wildlife

SEE: Chapter Nine, pages 104–115.

Illustrate the Lyrics to the Connecticut State Song

("Yankee Doodle")

Use markers, paints, photos, collages, colored pencils, or computer graphics to illustrate the lyrics to "Yankee Doodle," the state song. Turn your illustrations into a picture book, or scan them into PowerPoint and add music.

SEE: The lyrics to "Yankee Doodle" on page 128.

Research Connecticut's State Quarter

From 1999 to 2008, the U.S. Mint introduced new quarters commemorating each of the 50 states in the order that they were admitted to the Union. Each state's quarter features a unique design on its reverse, or back.

GO TO: www.factsfornow.scholastic.com. Enter the keyword **Connecticut** and look for the link to Connecticut quarter.

Research and write an essay explaining:

★ the significance of each image

★ who designed the quarter

★ who chose the final design

Design your own Connecticut state quarter. What images would you choose for the reverse?

Make a poster showing the Connecticut quarter and label each image.

SCIENCE, TECHNOLOGY, ENGINEERING, & MATH PROJECTS

Graph Population Statistics!

Compare population statistics (such as ethnic background, birth, death, and literacy rates) in Connecticut's counties or major cities. In your graph or chart, look at population density and write sentences describing what the population statistics show; graph one set of population statistics and write a paragraph explaining what the graphs reveal.

SEE: Chapter Six, pages 68–71.

Create a Weather Map of Connecticut!

Use your knowledge of Connecticut's geography to research and identify conditions that result in specific weather events. What is it about the geography of Connecticut that makes it vulnerable to things such as nor'easters? Create a weather map or poster that shows the weather patterns over the state. To accompany your map, explain the technology used to measure weather phenomena and provide data.

SEE: Chapter One, pages 13–15.

Barn owl

Track Endangered Species

Using your knowledge of Connecticut's wildlife, research what animals and plants are endangered or threatened. Find out what the state is doing to protect these species. Chart known populations of the animals and plants, and report on changes in certain geographic areas.

SEE: Chapter One, page 17.

PRIMARY VS. SECONDARY SOURCES

What's the Diff?

Your teacher may require at least one or two primary sources and one or two secondary sources for your assignment. So, what's the difference between the two?

★ **Primary sources are original.** You are reading the actual words of someone's diary, journal, letter, autobiography, or interview. Primary sources can also be photographs, maps, prints, cartoons, news/film footage, posters, first-person newspaper articles, drawings, musical scores, and recordings. By the way, when you conduct a survey, interview someone, shoot a video, or take photographs to include in a project, you are creating primary sources!

★ **Secondary sources are what you find in encyclopedias, textbooks, articles, biographies, and almanacs.** These are written by a person or group of people who tell about something that happened to someone else. Secondary sources also recount what another person said or did. This book is an example of a secondary source.

Now that you know what primary sources are—where can you find them?

★ **Your school or local library:** Check the library catalog for collections of original writings, government documents, musical scores, and so on. Some of this material may be stored on microfilm.

★ **Historical societies:** These organizations keep historical documents, photographs, and other materials. Staff members can help you find what you are looking for. History museums are also great places to see primary sources firsthand.

★ **The Internet:** There are lots of sites that have primary sources you can download and use in a project or assignment.

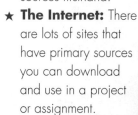

TIMELINE

★ ★ ★

U.S. Events **1600** **Connecticut Events**

1607
The first permanent English settlement is established in North America at Jamestown.

1614
Dutch explorer Adriaen Block sails up the Connecticut River.

1619
The first African indentured laborers in English North America are purchased for work in the Jamestown settlement.

1636
English settlers establish the colony.

1637
Pequots are massacred by an army of settlers and Mohegans during the Pequot War.

1638
English settlers establish the New Haven colony.

1639
The Fundamental Orders establish a democratic government in the Connecticut Colony.

1662
Connecticut Colony is granted a royal charter.

1665
Connecticut Colony and New Haven Colony unite into one colony.

Charter Oak

1682
René-Robert Cavelier, Sieur de La Salle, claims more than 1 million square miles (2.6 million sq km) of territory in the Mississippi River basin for France, naming it Louisiana.

1700

1701
Yale College is founded.

1756–1763
Connecticut troops fight in the French and Indian War.

U.S. Events

1776

Thirteen American colonies declare their independence from Great Britain.

1787

The U.S. Constitution is written.

1800

1812–15

The United States and Great Britain fight the War of 1812.

1830

The Indian Removal Act forces eastern Native American groups to relocate west of the Mississippi River.

1861–1865

The American Civil War is fought.

1866

The U.S. Congress approves the Fourteenth Amendment to the U.S. Constitution, granting citizenship to African Americans.

Connecticut Events

1775–1783

Connecticut takes part in the Revolutionary War. British troops attack Danbury, Greenwich, New Haven, Fairfield, Norwalk, and Forts Trumbull and Griswold.

1787

The Constitutional Convention in Philadelphia adopts the "Connecticut Compromise," which divides Congress into two chambers, the Senate and the House of Representatives.

1788

Connecticut becomes the fifth state to ratify the U.S. Constitution.

1793

Eli Whitney invents the cotton gin.

Cotton gin

1848

Slavery ends in Connecticut.

1852

Harriet Beecher Stowe publishes *Uncle Tom's Cabin*.

1855

Samuel Colt opens a gun factory in Hartford.

1861–1865

Connecticut troops fight in the American Civil War. State factories manufacture weapons and supplies.

124

U.S. Events `1900` Connecticut Events

1914–1918
Connecticut industries provide allies with weapons and supplies during World War I.

1917–18
The United States engages in World War I.

1920
The Nineteenth Amendment to the U.S. Constitution grants women the right to vote.

1929
The stock market crashes, plunging the United States more deeply into the Great Depression.

1930s
During the Great Depression, Governor Wilbur Cross creates jobs for the unemployed.

1941–45
The United States engages in World War II.

1941–1945
Connecticut industries boom, providing war materials during World War II.

1950–53
The United States engages in the Korean War.

1960s
Hartford is recognized as the insurance capital of the world.

1964–73
The United States engages in the Vietnam War.

1967–1968
Race riots in Bridgeport, Hartford, and others cities are sparked by civil unrest.

1974
Ella Grasso becomes the country's first woman to be elected a state governor.

Ella Grasso

`2000`

1981
African American Thirman Milner is elected mayor of Hartford.

2001
Terrorists hijack four U.S. aircraft and crash them into the World Trade Center in New York City, the Pentagon in Arlington, Virginia, and a Pennsylvania field, killing thousands.

2003
The United States and coalition forces invade Iraq.

2012
Hurricane Sandy slams into Connecticut.

GLOSSARY

bondage a state of being held against one's will

breechcloth a piece of cloth or leather worn at the lower body

constitution a set of laws organizing a government

convention a group of people meeting for a common purpose

depressed sunken or in a lower position

durable long-lasting

glacier a large moving body of ice

impressionist a style of making art that gives a sense or impression of the object or scene being depicted

insurance policy a written contract, or legal document, that guarantees a payment of money in case of loss of life, health, or property

interprets explains the meaning of

latitude the distance north or south of the earth's equator

militiamen members of a group of citizens organized for military duty

minuteman a member of a group who would fight at a minute's notice during the American Revolution

optics lenses, prisms, or mirrors used to aid one in seeing; found, for example, in glasses, microscopes, and telescopes

patent an official document giving only to an inventor the right to make, use, or sell the invention for a certain number of years

plantation an estate or farm where crops are planted

provision the act of providing, or a supply of needed materials

quarry a place where stone is dug

ratify approve officially

sinew the tough cord or tendon that connects muscles to bone

FAST FACTS

State Symbols

State seal

Statehood date	January 9, 1788, 5th
Origin of state name	From Algonquian words meaning "beside the long tidal river"
State capital	Hartford
State nicknames	Constitution State, Nutmeg State, the Provision State
State motto	*Qui Transtulit Sustinet* ("He who transplanted still sustains")
State bird	American robin
State flower	Mountain laurel
State animal	Sperm whale
State insect	Praying mantis
State mineral	Garnet
State song	"Yankee Doodle." See lyrics on page 128.
State tree	White Oak

Geography

Total area; rank	5,543 square miles (14,356 sq km); 48th
Land; rank	4,845 square miles (12,549 sq km); 48th
Water; rank	699 square miles (1,810 sq km); 37th
Inland water; rank	161 square miles (417 sq km); 47th
Coastal water; rank	538 square miles (1,393 sq km); 11th
Geographic center	Hartford, at East Berlin
Latitude	40° 58' N to 42° 3' N
Longitude	71° 47' W to 73° 44' W
Highest point	Mount Frissell, 2,380 feet (725 m)
Lowest point	Sea level at Long Island Sound
Largest city	Bridgeport
Number of counties	8
Longest river	Connecticut River

Population

Population; rank (2010 census)	3,574,097; 29th
Density (2010 census)	738 persons per square mile (285 per sq km)
Population distribution (2010 census)	88% urban, 12% rural
Race (2010 census)	White persons: 71.2%
	Black or African American persons: 9.4%
	Asian persons: 3.8%
	American Indian and Alaska Native persons: 0.2%
	Native Hawaiian and Other Pacific Islander persons: <0.1%
	Persons of two or more races: 1.7%
	Hispanic or Latino persons: 13.4%
	People of some other race: 0.3%

Weather

Record high temperature	106°F (41°C) at Torrington on August 23, 1916, and at Danbury on July 15, 1995
Record low temperature	−32°F (−36°C) at Falls Village on February 16, 1943, and at Coventry on January 22, 1961
Average July temperature	73°F (23°C)
Average January temperature	27°F (−3°C)
Average yearly precipitation	46 inches (117 cm)

State flag

STATE SONG

"Yankee Doodle"

The author of this song is unknown. During the Revolutionary War, however, Richard Shackburg gave the song to colonial soldiers.

Yankee Doodle went to town,
Riding on a pony,
Stuck a feather in his hat
And called it macaroni.

Yankee Doodle keep it up,
Yankee Doodle dandy,
Mind the music and the step,
And with the folks be handy.

NATURAL AREAS AND HISTORIC SITES

National Scenic Trails

Connecticut has two national scenic trails that run through it: the *Appalachian National Scenic Trail* and the *Connecticut Freedom Trail*, which includes sites associated with the *Amistad* revolt of 1839–1842 as well as buildings reported to have been used on the Underground Railroad.

National Heritage Corridor

Connecticut features a national heritage corridor, the *Quinebaug & Shetucket Rivers Valley National Heritage Corridor*. Visitors here have an opportunity to relax in a rural American setting and go to any number of the small, historic sites and towns that are included in this corridor.

National Historic Sites

Connecticut's *Weir Farm National Historic Site* in Wilton is named after the American Impressionist artist J. Alden Weir.

State Parks and Forests

Connecticut has a lovely state park system, featuring more than 60 beautiful state park areas, including the *Hammonasset Beach State Park*, the largest of the parks that border Long Island Sound; *Dinosaur State Park*, which has a giant dome that contains dinosaur tracks from 185 million years ago; *Talcott Mountain State Park*, which features Heublein Tower with a view of four states; and the *Putnam Memorial State Park*, which was the site of the Continental army's 1778–1779 winter encampment in Redding.

Hammonasset Beach State Park

SPORTS TEAMS

NCAA Teams (Division I)

Central Connecticut State *Blue Devils*
Fairfield University *Stags*
Quinnipiac University *Bobcats*
Sacred Heart University *Pioneers*
University of Connecticut *Huskies*
University of Hartford *Hawks*
Yale University *Bulldogs*

PROFESSIONAL SPORTS TEAMS

Women's National Basketball Association

Connecticut *Sun*

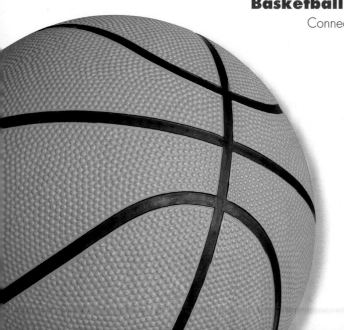

CULTURAL INSTITUTIONS

Libraries

The *Connecticut State Library* (Hartford) has several specialized collections, including the History and Genealogy Unit that provides access to historical materials about the state's citizens.

Yale University Library (New Haven) houses the Beinecke Rare Book and Manuscript Library and has extensive collections on African and Jewish cultures.

The *Connecticut Historical Society* is a library, museum, and education center. It is the seventh-oldest historical society in the nation.

Museums

The *Mark Twain House & Museum* (Hartford) includes the home where the famous American author lived in the late 1800s. The residence has many original furnishings and other personal belongings of Twain's family. The museum includes exhibit space, a library reading room, a shop, and a café.

The *Mashantucket Pequot Museum and Research Center* (Mashantucket) includes exhibits on the Mashantucket Pequot and other Native American groups.

Mystic Aquarium and Institute for Exploration (Mystic) includes exhibits on beluga whales, penguins, sea lions, and many other marine animals. Visitors can also experience what lies on the floors of the deep sea through interactive exhibits.

The *Wadsworth Atheneum* in Hartford is one of America's oldest public art museums. It has more than 50,000 pieces of art.

The *Yale Peabody Museum of Natural History* contains a 110-foot (34 m) mural called *The Age of Reptiles*, along with dinosaur bones in its Great Hall of Dinosaurs. The museum was founded in 1866.

Performing Arts

The *Connecticut Grand Opera and Orchestra* (Stamford) features world-class performances and talent from around the world.

The *Norwalk Symphony Orchestra* (Norwalk) offers live performances and educational activities to help people enjoy classical music.

Universities and Colleges

In 2013, Connecticut had 13 public and 29 private institutions of higher learning.

ANNUAL EVENTS

January–March

Connecticut Flower and Garden Show in Hartford (February)

Eastern States Ski Jumping Championships in Salisbury (February)

April–June

Daffodil Festival in Meriden (April)

Dogwood Festival in Fairfield (May)

Lobster Days in Mystic (May)

Barnum Festival in Bridgeport (June)

International Festival of Arts & Ideas in New Haven (June)

Farmington Antiques Weekend in Farmington (June)

July–September

Blessing of the Fleet in Stonington (early July)

Fife and Drum Ancient Muster Parade in Deep River (July)

Antique & Classic Boat Rendezvous in Mystic (July)

Riverfest in Hartford and East Hartford (July)

Sailfest in New London (July)

New Haven Open in New Haven (August)

Mystic Outdoor Art Festival in Mystic (August)

Norwalk Oyster Festival in Norwalk (September)

October–December

Garlic and Harvest Festival in Bethlehem (October)

Manchester Road Race in Manchester (November)

First Night Hartford in Hartford (December)

Christmas Torchlight Parade in Old Saybrook (December)

Dean Acheson (1893–1971) was a lawyer and statesman. While U.S. undersecretary of state, he developed the Truman Doctrine, a foreign policy plan, and helped establish the Marshall Plan, a foreign aid program. He served as U.S. secretary of state from 1949 to 1953. He was born in Middletown.

Ethan Allen (1738–1789) led the Green Mountain Boys in the capture of British Fort Ticonderoga in 1775 during the Revolutionary War. He was born in Litchfield.

Marian Anderson (1902–1993) was an African American singer who was denied permission to perform in 1939 because of her race. Instead, she performed before an audience of 75,000 at the Lincoln Memorial. She lived in Danbury.

Benedict Arnold (1741–1801) was an American general during the Revolutionary War who plotted to surrender the fort at West Point, New York. He joined the British army and has been regarded as an American traitor ever since. He was born in Norwich.

Phineas Taylor (P. T.) Barnum (1810–1891) helped found Ringling Brothers & Barnum and Bailey Circus. He was born in Bethel.

Henry Ward Beecher (1813–1887) was a powerful preacher at his Methodist church in Brooklyn, New York, and urged abolition of slavery. He was born in Litchfield.

P. T. Barnum

Richard Belzer (1944–) is a comedian and actor known for various roles, including that of Detective John Munch on TV's *Homicide: Life on the Street* and *Law & Order: Special Victims Unit*. He was born in Bridgeport.

James Blake (1979–) has been ranked as high as number two among professional American tennis players. He has a powerful forehand and is known for his speed. He attended high school in Fairfield.

John Brown (1800–1859) was an abolitionist who, at Harpers Ferry, Virginia, led a raid on the government arsenal in 1859. He was captured, tried, and hanged for treason. He was born in Torrington.

George H. W. Bush See page 91.

George W. Bush See page 91.

Marcus Camby (1974–) is a professional basketball player who has played for the Toronto Raptors, the New York Knicks, and the Denver Nuggets. He was born in Hartford.

Marcus Camby

Al Capp (1909–1979) was a cartoonist who created the *L'il Abner* cartoon strip. He was born Alfred Gerald Caplin in New Haven.

Karen Carpenter (1950–1982) and Richard Carpenter (1946–) were a musical sister-and-brother team who wrote and performed songs such as "We've Only Just Begun" and "Rainy Days and Mondays." Both were born in New Haven.

Lucia Chase (1897–1986) starred as a dancer in ballets such as *Petrouchka* and *Bluebeard*. Born in Waterbury, she founded the Ballet Theatre (now the American Ballet Theatre).

Roz Chast (1954–) is a cartoonist whose work appears in *The New Yorker* magazine. She lives in Ridgefield.

Samuel Clemens (1835–1910) is better known by his pen name Mark Twain. His books include *The Adventures of Tom Sawyer* and *The Adventures of Huckleberry Finn*, which were written while he lived in Hartford.

Glenn Close (1947–) has acted in numerous films including *The Big Chill*, *Fatal Attraction*, and *101 Dalmatians*. She was born in Greenwich.

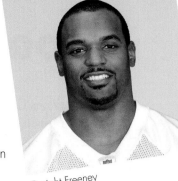

Thomas Cole See page 15.

Samuel Colt (1814–1862) invented the first successful repeating pistol in 1836. His gun factory in Hartford manufactured the Colt .45 revolver. He was born in Hartford.

Glenn Close

Prudence Crandall See page 49.

Lemuel R. Custis See page 60.

Thomas Dodd (1907–1971) served as an assistant to the U.S. attorney general between 1938 and 1945. He was a U.S. senator from Connecticut from 1959 to 1971. He was born in Norwich.

George Henry Durrie (1820–1863) was an artist who painted many Connecticut landscapes that later became Currier and Ives prints. He painted *Home for Thanksgiving*.

Oliver Ellsworth (1745–1807) was a lawyer and judge. He served in the Continental Congress from 1777 to 1784 and was a delegate to the Constitutional Convention in 1787. He served as chief justice of the U.S. Supreme Court from 1796 to 1800. He was born in Windsor.

Dwight Freeney

Dwight Freeney (1980–) is a professional football player who has played as a defensive end for the Indianapolis Colts. He was born in Hartford.

Thomas Hopkins Gallaudet (1797–1851) was a teacher who founded America's first free school for the deaf in Hartford in 1817.

Elizabeth George (1894–1973) was a Pequot activist who helped save Native land in Connecticut.

William Gillette See page 59.

Charles Goodyear See page 54.

Ella Grasso See page 90.

Nathan Hale (1755–1776) was a teacher and patriot whose last words, "I regret that I have but one life to lose for my country," won him lasting fame. He was born in Coventry.

Matt Harvey (1989–) is a pitcher for baseball's New York Mets. Born in New London, he was a star ballplayer at the University of North Carolina. In his first full season in the Major Leagues, in 2013, he was selected the National League's starting pitcher in the All-Star Game.

Katharine Hepburn (1907–2003) was born in Hartford. The only person to win four Academy Awards for acting, Hepburn won Oscars for her work in the films *Morning Glory*, *Guess Who's Coming to Dinner*, *The Lion in Winter*, and *On Golden Pond*.

Thomas Hooker (1586–1647) was an early settler and religious leader who helped draft the *Fundamental Orders of 1639*.

Isaac Hull (1773–1843) was a naval officer who commanded the USS *Constitution* ("Old Ironsides"). He was born in Derby.

Charles Edward Ives (1874–1954) was a composer who received the 1947 Pulitzer Prize in music for his *Symphony No. 3*. He was born in Danbury.

Edward Calvin Kendall (1886–1972) shared the 1950 Nobel Prize in Medicine for his research on adrenal cortex hormones. He was born in Norwalk.

John Frederick Kensett (1816–1872) was a well-known landscape artist. He was born in Cheshire.

Eriq La Salle (1962–) is an actor best known for his roles in the film *Coming to America* and on TV's *ER*. He was born in Hartford.

Eriq La Salle

Norman Lear (1922–) is a television producer who created *All in the Family*, *Maude*, and *The Jeffersons*. He was born in New Haven.

Joe Lieberman (1942–) was a U.S. senator from Connecticut from 1989 to 2013. He previously served as attorney general of the state from 1983 to 1989. Lieberman was the Democratic Party's vice presidential nominee in 2000, with Al Gore as his running mate seeking the office of president. George W. Bush and his running mate, Dick Cheney, defeated them.

Kristine Lilly (1971–) has been a longtime member of the U.S. women's national soccer team. She won Olympic gold medals for team competition in 1996 and 2004. She grew up in Wilton.

Kristine Lilly

Rebecca Lobo (1973–) played professional women's basketball in the Women's National Basketball Association from 1997 to 2003. She was also a member of the University of Connecticut's 1995 national championship basketball team. Today, she appears as a sports reporter for ESPN.

Clare Boothe Luce (1903–1987) was a playwright, politician, and diplomat. Her plays include *Abide With Me* and *Margin for Error*. She served Connecticut as a member of the U.S. House of Representatives from 1943 to 1947 and was U.S. ambassador to Italy from 1953 to 1956.

John Mayer (1977–) is a singer, songwriter, and guitarist. He has won Grammy Awards for his songs "Your Body Is a Wonderland" and "Waiting on the World to Change." He was born in Fairfield.

Barbara McClintock (1902–1992) was a biologist who received the 1983 Nobel Prize in Medicine. She was born in Hartford.

Seth McFarlane (1973–) is the creator of the TV show *Family Guy* and co-creator of *American Dad!* and *The Cleveland Show.* Born in Kent, he studied art and illustration at the Rhode Island School of Design. He often provides the voices for characters in his animated shows.

Thirman Milner See page 63.

Thirman Milner

Moby (born Richard Melville Hall, 1965–) is a musician known for his electronic music and support of animal rights. He achieved international success for the album *Play,* which sold more than 10 million records worldwide within a year. He grew up in Darien.

John Pierpont (J. P.) Morgan (1837–1913) was a banker and investor. A multimillionaire, he collected many valuable paintings, sculptures, books, and letters, and later donated them to libraries and museums. He was born in Hartford.

Ralph Nader (1934–) is a consumer advocate and politician. In 2000 and 2004, he was an independent candidate for U.S. president. He was born in Winsted.

Frederick Law Olmsted (1822–1903) was a landscape architect who designed the U.S. Capitol grounds, Connecticut's capitol grounds, New York City's Central Park, and many other sites. He was born in Hartford.

Eugene O'Neill

Eugene O'Neill See page 80.

Carrie Saxon Perry See page 64.

Liz Phair (1967–) is a singer and guitarist whose CD *Exile in Guyville* was honored as one of *Rolling Stone*'s best 500 albums of all time. She was born in New Haven.

Gifford Pinchot See page 16.

Adam Clayton Powell Jr. (1908–1972), born in New Haven, was an African American member of the U.S. House of Representatives from 1945 to 1971, representing Harlem in New York City.

Israel Putnam (1718–1790) served as a major general in the Continental army, commanding American troops at the Battle of Bunker Hill in 1775. He lived in Pomfret.

Abraham Ribicoff (1910–1998) served as a Connecticut congressman and governor, as well as a U.S. senator from Connecticut from 1963 to 1981. He was born in New Britain.

Paul Robeson See page 79.

Jackie Robinson (1919–1972) was the first African American baseball player to play for a major league team. In 1947, he joined the Brooklyn Dodgers and had a long and distinguished career. He lived in Stamford.

Rosalind Russell (1912–1976) was an actor who received four Academy Award nominations during her career. She was born in Waterbury.

Maurice Sendak (1928–2012) was a writer and illustrator of children's books. His best-known work is *Where the Wild Things Are*, a story about a boy who goes to a faraway island and has adventures with strange animals. The story has been made into an opera, a cartoon, and a live-action movie. Sendak was born in New York City and lived in Connecticut for many years.

Roger Sherman (1721–1793) was a signer of the Declaration of Independence and the U.S. Constitution. He lived in New Milford.

Igor Sikorsky See page 99.

Benjamin Spock (1903–1998) was a doctor who specialized in baby care. He was born in New Haven.

Wallace Stevens See page 78.

Harriet Beecher Stowe (1811–1896) was a novelist and abolitionist. Born in Litchfield, she wrote *Uncle Tom's Cabin*, which detailed the brutality of slavery.

John Trumbull (1756–1843) painted dramatic scenes of the Revolutionary War, several of which hang in the U.S. Capitol. He was born in Lebanon.

Jonathan Trumbull (1710–1785) was a politician and patriot. He was born in Lebanon.

Mo Vaughn (1967–) was a professional baseball player who played first base for the Boston Red Sox, the Anaheim Angels, and the New York Mets. Born in Norwalk, he was named American League MVP in 1995 and retired from the game in 2003.

Mo Vaughn

Noah Webster (1758–1843) is best known as the creator of the Merriam-Webster dictionary, which was first published in 1828. Born in New Hartford, he graduated from Yale University and later served in the Connecticut Militia during the Revolutionary War.

Gideon Welles (1802–1878) served as U.S. secretary of the navy from 1861 to 1869. He was born in Glastonbury.

Eli Whitney (1765–1825) invented the cotton gin in 1793. He attended Yale University in New Haven.

Harriet Beecher Stowe

RESOURCES

BOOKS

Nonfiction

Bodden, Valerie. *Mark Twain*. Minneapolis, Minn.: ABDO Publishing, 2013.

Cunningham, Kevin. *The Connecticut Colony*. New York: Children's Press, 2012.

Elliot, Henry. *Harriet Beecher Stowe: The Voice of Humanity in White America*. New York: Crabtree, 2010.

Gibson, Karen Bush. *Native American History for Kids: With 21 Activities*. Chicago: Chicago Review Press, 2010.

La Bella, Laura. *Connecticut: Past and Present*. New York: Rosen Central. 2011.

Slavicek, Louise Chipley. *Paul Robeson: Entertainer and Activist*. New York: Chelsea House, 2011.

Fiction

Avi. *Windcatcher*. New York: Bradbury, 1991.

Collier, James Lincoln. *The Bloody Country*. New York: Four Winds, 1976.

Collier, James Lincoln. *The Clock*. New York: Delacorte, 1992.

Collier, James Lincoln. *My Brother Sam Is Dead*. New York: Simon and Schuster, 1984.

Janeczko, Paul. *Worlds Afire: The Hartford Circus Fire of 1944*. New York: Candlewick, 2004.

Monjo, F. N. *The Secret of the Sachem's Tree*. New York: Coward, McCann & Geoghegan, 1972.

Pinkney, Andrea Davis. *Hold Fast to Dreams*. New York: Morrow, 1995.

Speare, Elizabeth George. *The Witch of Blackbird Pond*. New York: Collins, 2003.

Twain, Mark. *A Connecticut Yankee in King Arthur's Court*. New York: Signet Classics, 2004.

Visit this Scholastic Web site for more information on Connecticut:
www.factsfornow.scholastic.com
Enter the keyword **Connecticut**

FACTS FOR NOW

INDEX

★ ★ ★

AUTHOR'S TIPS AND SOURCE NOTES

★ ★ ★

In addition to visiting Connecticut over the years, I made use of many books during my research. Connecticut travel books were especially helpful. These included *Off the Beaten Path: Connecticut* by David and Deborah Ritchie, *Connecticut: An Explorer's Guide Connecticut* by Barnett D. Laschever and Andi Marie Cantele, and *Connecticut & Rhode Island* by Anna Mundow. Many history books were also of great value, including *Mainstream and Ebb: Readings in the Geography of Connecticut* by Thomas R. Lewis, *Connecticut* by David M. Roth, *The New England Indians* by C. Keith Wilbur, *Puritans against the Wilderness* by Albert E. Van Dusen, *American Yesterday* by Eric Sloane, and *A Diverse People: Connecticut, 1914 to the Present* by Herbert F. Janick.

For recent articles about Connecticut, I relied on microfilm copies of the *New York Times*. The *Times* provided me with excellent political and social information about the state.

Of course, I made much use of the Internet. There are too many fine Web sites about Connecticut to list. There is plenty to learn about Connecticut, and there are plenty of interesting sources where you can find information about it.